BY LESLIE MARMON SILKO

YELLOW WOMAN AND A BEAUTY OF THE SPIRIT (ESSAYS)

SACRED WATER (AUTOBIOGRAPHY)

ALMANAC OF THE DEAD (A NOVEL)

STORYTELLER (SHORT STORIES)

CEREMONY (A NOVEL)

LAGUNA WOMAN (COLLECTION OF VERSE)

YELLOW WOMAN AND A BEAUTY OF THE SPIRIT

ESSAYS ON
NATIVE AMERICAN
LIFE TODAY

LESLIE MARMON SILKO

SIMON & SCHUSTER
NEW YORK LONDON TORONTO
SYDNEY TOKYO SINGAPORE

SIMON & SCHUSTER
ROCKEFELLER CENTER
1230 AVENUE OF THE AMERICAS
NEW YORK, NY 10020

DESIGNED BY BARBARA MARKS

MANUFACTURED IN THE UNITED STATES OF AMERICA

10 9 8 7 6 5 4 3 2 1

LIBRARY OF CONGRESS CATALOGING-IN-PUBLICATION DATA
SILKO, LESLIE, DATE.
YELLOW WOMAN AND A BEAUTY OF THE SPIRIT :
ESSAYS ON NATIVE AMERICAN LIFE TODAY / LESLIE
MARMON SILKO.
P. CM.
INCLUDES BIBLIOGRAPHICAL REFERENCES.
1. INDIAN PHILOSOPHY. 2. INDIANS—FOLKLORE.
3. INDIANS—SOCIAL CONDITIONS. I. TITLE.
R59.P45S55 1996
970.004'97—DC20 96-38895 CIP
ISBN 0-684-81153-7

TO

MARY VIRGINIA LESLIE,
MY MOTHER

AND

LELAND HOWARD MARMON,
MY FATHER

Contents

YELLOW WOMAN AND A BEAUTY OF THE SPIRIT

Introduction

In the early 1980s, as I was beginning to write *Almanac of the Dead,* I began a series of short prose pieces about the desert area around my house, and about the rocks, and about the rain that is so precious to this land and to my household, which still depends on wells for all its water. In 1980 I had also begun to take photographs of the rocks in the big wash by my house; I used black-and-white and color film, and Polaroid film as well. I began collecting newspaper clippings and magazine articles about rocks that ran amok, and about meteorites that fell through roofs. I began to save articles about rain, about the El Niño weather systems that cause floods in some areas and droughts in others. I began assembling piles of notes I had made on rocks and on rain. I intended to write two long essays, one on rain and one on rocks.

I have continued to gather and hoard piles of notes and articles for my essays. I imagined my essays as perfect pieces, and I did not want to hurry them. I set the notes and incomplete essays aside while I completed *Almanac.* I recall a section of the novel in which there are descriptions of the peculiar rocks in the Tucson Mountains, and another in which meteorites are a central focus.

But in the meantime, I got requests to write essays, and sometimes, if the topic interested me, I would agree. Later, as I toiled over bland prose and argued with magazine editors, I would regret that I had ever agreed to write nonfiction, and I would swear off nonfiction prose forever. But secretly I hoped that the struggle with these other pieces of nonfiction would empower me to bring forth my essays on rain and on rocks. Instead, the writing of these other essays has had an unexpected effect on my essays about rain and about rocks, as you will see in the last section of this book.

In my 1993 self-published book, *Sacred Water,* photocopies of my photographs of clouds and dry washes are integral to the text: the images are as much a part of my essay on water as are the words. The Pueblo people have always connected certain stories with certain locations; it is these places that give the narratives such resonance over the centuries. The Pueblo people and the land and the stories are inseparable. In the creation of the text itself, I see no reason to separate visual images from written words that are visual images themselves.

As I learned more about the ancient folding books of the Maya, Aztec, and other indigenous American cultures, I began to think more about the written word as a picture of the spoken word. I began to contemplate writing an essay in which the written words depended upon visual images, or pictures, to fully express what I had to say.

Grandma Lily kept a tall Hopi basket full of old family snapshots. Sometimes we did not move the Hopi basket for months, but then Grandpa Hank or Grandma Lily would be talking about someone or about something that had happened a long time ago, and down came the Hopi basket, full to the top with old black-and-white and even a few sepia photographs. We children would look intently at the faces, study the clothing, and always we looked for any indication of landscape to tell us if the photograph was taken around Laguna. The hills in the background remained the same, and even as a child I was thrilled with that notion—the donkey and horses and wagons and the people dressed so oddly all had changed, but Beacon Hill and Pa'toe'che remained the same.

When I was four years old I began to climb over the fence and leave the yard where I was supposed to stay. Our house was at the bottom of the hill, by the road everyone took to the post office and store. I watched for people to pass by and I would talk to them; the older kids would tell me all kinds of wild stories because I believed what they told me and I got so excited. I could hear the drumming from the plaza whenever there were ceremonial dances, and I always wanted to go because everyone was gathered around the plaza and the dancers were so powerful to watch.

One day the older kids told me that there were special dancers up at the plaza, and these dancers ate wood. I still remember climbing over the fence, because it was a four-foot-high fence but the wire had good spaces to put my feet. I walked quite a distance before Marsalina Thompson saw me. In those days, everyone watched out for everyone else's children, especially the little ones. Marsalina saw me and she knew that I wasn't supposed to be marching along by myself, so she brought me home. I cried and cried and tried to tell her that I must get to the plaza to see the amazing dancers who ate wood, but she was firm.

I was never afraid to go anywhere around Laguna when I was growing up. I was never afraid of any person unless the person was an outsider. Outsiders were white people, mostly tourists who drove up and did not stay long. But up in the sandhills and among the sandstone formations around Laguna, I did not see many Laguna people either, only people cutting wood or returning from their sheep camp. Up in the hills with the birds and animals and my horse, I felt absolutely safe; I knew outsiders and kidnappers stayed out of the hills. I spent hours and hours alone in the hills southeast of Laguna. After I got my beloved horse, Joey, and before I had to work so much at my grandpa's store, I often spent all day on my horse, riding all around old Laguna. The old folks who did not know my name would refer to me as "the little girl on the horse." I was perfectly happy, lost in my thoughts and imagination as I rode my horse.

Sometimes I stopped, tied up my horse, and investigated interesting petroglyphs on sandstone cliffs or searched for arrowheads in the ruins of older settlements. I preferred to be without human companions so I could give my complete attention to the hills. Of course, from the time I can remember, I preferred to play alone with my little figures of farm animals, cowboys, and Indians because I liked to make up elaborate dramas in which I whispered what each of the characters was saying; the presence of my sisters and other playmates inhibited these dramas. I was a tomboy who liked to climb cottonwood trees and wade in the river. For real adventure I used to tag along with Gary Fernandez, who was my age, and we would try to keep up with Gary's older brother Ron and his pal Mike Trujillo. The older boys would let us follow for a while before they ditched us.

Because our family was such a mixture of Indian, Mexican, and white, I was acutely aware of the inherent conflicts between Indian and white, old-time beliefs and Christianity. But from the start, I had no use for Christianity because the Christians made up such terrible lies about Indian people that it was clear to me they would lie about other matters also. My beloved Grandma A'mooh was a devout Presbyterian, but I can remember, even as a little girl, listening to her read from the Bible and thinking, "I love her with all my heart, but I don't believe in the Bible." I spent time with Aunt Susie and with Grandpa Hank, who was not a Christian. The mesas and hills loved me; the Bible meant punishment. Life at Laguna for me was a daily balancing act of Laguna beliefs and Laguna ways and the ways of the outsiders. No wonder I preferred to wander in the hills by myself, on my horse, Joey, with Bulls-eye, my dog.

Grandma Lily took me and my sisters on walks to the river, and as we got older, she took us to hike in the mesas and sandhills as she had done with my father and his brothers when they were young. She wasn't afraid of anything in the hills; she was the horsewoman who would ride any bronco, and she wore a woman's dress and women's shoes only three times a year, to Mass on Christmas Eve and for Palm Sunday and Easter Sunday.

I have always felt safer alone in the hills than I feel when I am around people. Humans are the most dangerous of all animals, that's what my mother said. She was fearless with snakes and picked up rattlesnakes with ease. Most of my life I have lived in small settlements or I have lived outside of town, as I do now, in the hills outside of Tucson, where the nearest house is a quarter mile away. I still trust the land—the rocks, the shrubs, the cactus, the rattlesnakes, and mountain lions—far more than I trust human beings. I never feel lonely when I walk alone in the hills: I am surrounded with living beings, with these sandstone ridges and lava rock hills full of life. Luckily I enjoy danger, so I find human beings irresistible; humans are natural forces, just like flash floods or blizzards.

I was only five or six years old when my father was elected tribal treasurer. During his term, the Pueblo of Laguna filed a big lawsuit against the state of New Mexico for six million acres of land the state wrongfully took. The land had been granted by the king of Spain to the Pueblo hundreds of years before the United States even existed, let alone the state of New Mexico. The lawyer hired by Pueblo of Laguna and the expert witnesses, archaeologists, used to meet at our house to prepare to testify in court.

What made the strongest impression on me, though, were the old folks who also were expert witnesses. For months the old folks and Aunt Susie met twice a week after supper at our house to go over the testimony. Many of them were so aged they could hardly get around; Aunt Susie seemed spry compared to them. She interpreted English for the old folks because she knew them very well; in her own studies of Laguna history she had talked with them many times. Now she helped them prepare their testimony, that from time immemorial the Kawakemeh, the people of the Pueblo of Laguna, had been sustained from hunting and planting on this land stolen by the state of New Mexico. It was explained to me that the old folks testified with stories—stories of childhood outings with adults to gather piñons or to haul wood, stories they had heard as children. The old folks were going up against the state of New Mexico with only the stories.

The land claims lawsuit made a great and lasting impression on me. I heard the old folks cry as they talked about the land and how it had been taken from them. To them the land was as dear as a child, and as I listened, I felt the loss and the anger too, as if it all had happened only yesterday.

When I was a sophomore in high school I decided law school was the place to seek justice. I majored in English at the University of New Mexico only because I loved to read and write about what I'd read. Sure, I wrote short stories and I'd received a little discovery grant from the National Endowment for the Arts, but my destination was law school, where I planned to learn how to obtain justice. I should have paid more attention to the lesson of the Laguna Pueblo land claims lawsuit from my childhood: The lawsuit was not settled until I was in law school. The U.S. Court of Indian Claims found in favor of the Pueblo of Laguna, but the Indian Claims Court never gives back land wrongfully taken; the court only pays tribes for the land. The amount paid is computed without interest according to the value of the land at the time it was taken. The Laguna people wanted the land they cherished; instead, they got twenty-five cents for each of the six million acres stolen by the state. The lawsuit had lasted twenty years, so the lawyers' fees amounted to nearly $2 million.

I completed three semesters in the American Indian Law School Fellowship Program before I realized that injustice is built into the Anglo-American legal system. Professor Jerome Walden taught our first-year law class the history of the Anglo-American legal system. He assigned Dickens's *Bleak House* as one of our texts, but long before Dickens's greedy lawyers consumed the entire estate of the Jarndyce family, I could read between the lines: the feudal lord with all the money and all the power who doles out justice to his serfs and vassals is the model for our modern-day judges. The

Anglo-American legal system was designed by and for the feudal lords; to this day, money and power deliver "justice" only to the rich and powerful; it cannot do otherwise.

But I continued in law school until our criminal law class read an appeal to the U.S. Supreme Court to stop the execution of a retarded black man convicted of strangling a white librarian in Washington, D.C., in 1949. The majority on the court refused to stop the execution, though it was clear that the man was so retarded that he had no comprehension of his crime. That case was the breaking point for me. I wanted nothing to do with such a barbaric legal system.

My time in law school was not wasted: I had gained invaluable insights into the power structure of mainstream society, and I continue to follow developments in the law to calculate prevailing political winds. It seems to me there is no better way to uncover the deepest values of a culture than to observe the operation of that culture's system of justice.

I decided the only way to seek justice was through the power of the stories. I left law school and enrolled in a beginning photography class and a couple of graduate courses in the English department. I was already thinking about how one might combine text and photographs so that on the page there is a coherent whole, rather than two competing entities. One of the classes I took examined the interrelationship between William Blake's texts and the illuminated pages they appear on. But I wanted to make these texts, not just study them, so I dropped the class. I was happy to leave the university, in 1971, to go live and teach on the Navajo reservation at Chinle. I first had seen the mighty sandstone cliffs of Canyon de Chelly and Canyon del Muerto when I was fourteen, and it was wonderful to be there. I learned a great deal from my students and from my neighbors in Chinle and Many Farms, as I realized later on when I wrote my novel

Ceremony. I made a makeshift darkroom in the bathroom and I kept taking pictures; someday I was going to make a text with my words and my pictures.

THIS BOOK OF essays is structured like a spider's web. It begins with the land; think of the land, the earth, as the center of a spider's web. Human identity, imagination and storytelling were inextricably linked to the land, to Mother Earth, just as the strands of the spider's web radiate from the center of the web.

From the spoken word, or storytelling, comes the written word, as well as the visual image. The next part of this book is caught up with representation and visualization of narrative, of storytelling; Mayan folding books, murals, and finally photography with narrative are explored. The rich visual languages of the Aztec and Maya codices, or folding books, are closely related to the great frescoes, or mural paintings, of the Maya and Aztec pyramids. Similar massive frescoes are found on the walls of kivas in ancient Pueblo towns.

Except for a few fragments, the magnificent folding books of the Maya and Aztec people were destroyed in 1540 by Bishop Landa, who burned the great libraries of the Americas. Europeans were anxious to be rid of all evidence that Native American cultures were intellectually equal to European cultures; they could then argue to the pope that these indigenous inhabitants were not fully human and that Europeans were therefore free to do with them and their land as they pleased.

The books were destroyed and the people who knew how to make the books were destroyed. Soon the only books of Native American life were written and made by non-Indians, who continued to portray indigenous people as subhumans. The U.S. government used books in their campaign of cultural genocide. Thus the representation or portrayal of Native Americans was politicized from the very beginning and, to this day, remains an explosive political issue.

The final section of this book is my favorite, because here is the "Black Rock" section excerpted from my new work in progress, "An Essay on Rocks." Here the text and photographs create a slightly different syntax for the page.

Around 1975, the *Chicago Review* published an issue that had no text at all, only photographs that narrated a story about a lovely old farm house, two women and two men, and the ghost of a nude woman. The notion of using only photographs to tell a short story was just what I had been thinking about; the only problem with the *Chicago Review*'s experiment had been the weak story they had chosen to tell.

In 1976, living back at Laguna, I bought a wonderful Toyo field camera designed for easy backpacking into the hills. I loved the meditative mood I was in by the time I had completed the painstaking setup of the tripod and camera. This process seemed to me a ritual, a sort of prayer to the horizon or mountains I loved and desired in my photography.

After I moved to Tucson in 1978, I felt a need for change. I bought an autofocus 35mm camera for $99; I didn't want to have to think about aperture and shutter speeds or even focusing, because those technical details made me self-conscious and my photographs had no spontaneity. This camera was perfect because I didn't have to think about what I was doing; I had only to point this little camera and snap whenever something caught my eye. I wanted my subconscious self to take the pictures. I was curious to see what, if anything, my subconscious could do with a camera. I shot the first roll of thirty-six as rapidly as I could over two or three days. I didn't think my experiment was working, because all I could remember was pointing and shooting at odd, unrelated subjects: a black sedan parked in the wash below my house, a giant spider's web glistening over desert weeds, and a strange pile of rocks.

I took the film to the drugstore for processing because I had decided that I would allow all the variables to come into play, just to see what happened. I didn't expect much. But when I began looking at the prints, I was amazed to see that the photographs did indeed tell a story. The black sedan parked in the dry wash had not seemed remarkable to me the day I photographed it. But now, in the black-and-white photograph, the car's presence was sinister and full of foreboding. The big silvery spider's web glistening on low weeds no longer looked like itself; now it appeared to outline a depression in the ground that might have been a shallow grave. The advent of *Almanac of the Dead* can be traced to this roll of film; a recurring image in *Almanac* is the shallow grave that I took from this early photo-narrative, titled "The Shallow Grave."

I photographed nonstop with my rinky-dink camera all of 1980 and 1981. After I began to work in earnest on *Almanac,* I did not make as many photographs as in previous years, but I kept working with the camera. I began photographing the big wash near my house. I began to photograph the rocks because they moved and changed with each rainstorm. About this time I became intrigued with the electronic photography of copying machines, and when I wasn't working on *Almanac,* I experimented printing my photographs on a black-and-white copying machine. I liked the way the machine prints minimalized the dominance of the photographic image on the page.

I have wanted to work with my photographs and my essays on rocks and on rain since this time, and finally, last year, I completed "An Essay on Rocks," which is an excerpt from the longer work now in progress. This is the direction my essays have taken, and I could not be more happy than I am, coaxing the photographs and the narratives to work as one. As I sit here and type this sentence, lavender-blue nimbus clouds are drifting in from the southwest off the Gulf of California; by tomorrow there may be rain. I can hardly wait to return to my photographs of clouds and my essay on rain.

Interior and Exterior Landscapes: The Pueblo Migration Stories

From a High Arid Plateau in New Mexico

You see that, after a thing is dead, it dries up. It might take weeks or years, but eventually, if you touch the thing, it crumbles under your fingers. It goes back to dust. The soul of the thing has long since departed. With the plants and wild game the soul may have already been born back into bones and blood or thick green stalks and leaves. Nothing is wasted. What cannot be eaten by people or in some way used must then be left where other living creatures may benefit. What domestic animals or wild scavengers can't eat will be fed to the plants. The plants feed on the dust of these few remains.

The ancient Pueblo people buried the dead in vacant rooms or in partially collapsed rooms adjacent to the main living quarters. Sand and clay, used to construct the roof, make layers many inches deep once the roof has collapsed. The layers of sand and clay make for easy grave digging. The vacant room fills with cast-off objects and debris. When a vacant room has filled deep enough, a shallow but adequate grave can be scooped in a far corner. Archaeologists have remarked over formal burials complete with elaborate funerary objects excavated in trash middens of abandoned rooms. But the rocks and adobe mortar of collapsed walls were valued by the ancient people, because each rock had been carefully selected for size and shape, then chiseled to an even face. Even the pink clay adobe melting with each rainstorm had to be prayed over, then dug and carried some distance. Corncobs and husks, the rinds and stalks and animal bones were not regarded by the ancient people as filth or garbage. The remains were merely resting at a midpoint in their journey back to dust. Human remains are not so different. They should rest with the bones and rinds where they all may benefit living creatures—small rodents and insects—until their return is completed. The remains of things—animals and plants, the clay and stones—were treated with respect, because for the ancient people all these things had spirit and being.[1]

The antelope merely consents to return home with the hunter. All phases of the hunt are conducted with love: the love the hunter and the people have for the Antelope People, and the love of the antelope who agree to give up their meat and blood so that human beings will not starve. Waste of meat or even the thoughtless handling of bones cooked bare will offend the antelope spirits. Next year the hunters will vainly search the dry plains for antelope. Thus, it is necessary to return carefully the bones and hair and the stalks and leaves to the earth, who first created them. The spirits remain close by. They do not leave us.

The dead become dust, and in this becoming they are once more joined with the Mother. The ancient Pueblo people called the earth the Mother Creator of all things in this world. Her sister, the Corn Mother, occasionally merges with her because all succulent green life rises out of the depths of the earth.

Rocks and clay are part of the Mother. They emerge in various forms, but at some time before they were smaller particles of great boulders. At a later time they may again become what they once were: dust.

A rock shares this fate with us and with animals and plants as well. A rock has being or spirit, although we may not understand it. The spirit may differ from the spirit we know in animals or plants or in ourselves. In the end we all originate from the depths of the earth. Perhaps this is how all beings share in the spirit of the Creator. We do not know.

FROM THE EMERGENCE PLACE

PUEBLO POTTERS, THE creators of petroglyphs and oral narratives, never conceived of removing themselves from the earth and sky. So long as the human consciousness remains *within* the hills, canyons, cliffs, and the plants, clouds, and sky, the term *landscape,* as it has entered the English language, is misleading. "A portion of territory the eye can comprehend in a single view" does not correctly describe the relationship between the human being and his or her surroundings. This assumes the viewer is somehow *outside* or *separate from* the territory she or he surveys. Viewers are as much a part of the landscape as the boulders they stand on.

There is no high mesa edge or mountain peak where one can stand and not immediately be part of all that surrounds. Human identity is linked with all the elements of creation through the clan; you might belong to the Sun Clan or the Lizard Clan or the Corn Clan or the Clay Clan.[2] Standing deep within the natural world, the ancient Pueblo understood the thing as it was—the squash blossom, grasshopper, or rabbit itself could never be created by the human hand. Ancient Pueblos took the modest view that the thing itself (the landscape) could not be improved upon. The ancients did not presume to tamper with what had already been created. Thus *realism,* as we now recognize it in painting and sculpture, did not catch the imaginations of Pueblo people until recently.

The squash blossom itself is *one thing:* itself. So the ancient Pueblo potter abstracts what she saw to be the key elements of the squash blossom—the four symmetrical petals, with four symmetrical stamens in the center. These key elements, while suggesting the squash flower, also link it with the four cardinal directions. Represented only in its intrinsic form, the squash flower is released from a limited meaning or restricted identity. Even in the most sophisticated abstract form, a squash flower or a cloud or a lightning bolt became intricately connected with a complex system of relationships that the ancient Pueblo people maintained with each other and with the populous natural world they lived within. A bolt of lightning is itself, but at the same time it may mean much more. It may be a messenger of good fortune when summer rains are needed. It may deliver death, perhaps the result of manipulations by the Gunnadeyahs, destructive necromancers. Lightning may strike down an evildoer, or lightning may strike a person of goodwill. If the person survives, lightning endows him or her with heightened power.

Pictographs and petroglyphs of constellations or elk or

antelope draw their magic in part from the process wherein the focus of all prayer and concentration is upon the thing itself, which, in its turn, guides the hunter's hand. Connection with the spirit dimensions requires a figure or form that is all-inclusive. A lifelike rendering of an elk is too restrictive. Only the elk *is* itself. A *realistic* rendering of an elk would be only one particular elk anyway. The purpose of the hunt rituals and magic is to make contact with *all* the spirits of the elk.

The land, the sky, and all that is within them—the landscape—includes human beings. Interrelationships in the Pueblo landscape are complex and fragile. The unpredictability of the weather, the aridity and harshness of much of the terrain in the high plateau country explain in large part the relentless attention the ancient Pueblo people gave to the sky and the earth around them. Survival depended upon harmony and cooperation not only among human beings, but also among all things—the animate and the less animate, since rocks and mountains were known on occasion to move.

The ancient Pueblos believed the Earth and the Sky were sisters (or sister and brother in the post-Christian version). As long as food-family relations are maintained, then the Sky will continue to bless her sister, the Earth, with rain, and the Earth's children will continue to survive. But the old stories recall incidents in which troublesome spirits or beings threaten the earth. In one story, a malicious *ka'tsina,* called the Gambler, seizes the Shiwana, or Rain Clouds, the Sun's beloved children.[3] The Shiwana are snared in magical power late one afternoon on a high mountaintop. The Gambler takes the Rain Clouds to his mountain stronghold, where he locks them in the north room of his house. What was his idea? The Shiwana were beyond value. They brought life to all things on earth. The Gambler wanted a big stake to wager in his games of chance. But such greed, even on the part of only one being, had the effect of threatening the survival of all life on earth. Sun Youth, aided by old Grandmother Spider, outsmarts the Gambler and the rigged game, and the Rain Clouds are set free. The drought ends, and once more life thrives on earth.

THROUGH THE STORIES WE HEAR WHO WE ARE

ALL SUMMER THE people watch the west horizon, scanning the sky from south to north for rain clouds. Corn must have moisture at the time the tassels form. Otherwise pollination will be incomplete, and the ears will be stunted and shriveled. An inadequate harvest may bring disaster. Stories told at Hopi, Zuñi, and at Acoma and Laguna describe drought and starvation as recently as 1900. Precipitation in west-central New Mexico averages fourteen inches annually. The western pueblos are located at altitudes over 5,600 feet above sea level, where winter temperatures at night fall below freezing. Yet evidence of their presence in the high desert and plateau country goes back ten thousand years. The ancient Pueblo not only survived in this environment, but for many years they also thrived. In A.D. 1100 the people at Chaco Canyon had built cities with apartment buildings of stone five stories high.[4] Their sophistication as sky watchers was surpassed only by Mayan and Inca astronomers. Yet this vast complex of knowledge and belief, amassed for thousands of years, was never recorded in writing.

Instead, the ancient Pueblo people depended upon collective memory through successive generations to maintain and transmit an entire culture, a worldview complete with proven strategies for survival. The oral narrative, or story, became the medium through which the complex of Pueblo knowledge and belief was maintained. Whatever the event or the subject, the ancient people perceived the world and themselves within that world as part of an ancient, continuous story composed of innumerable bundles of other stories.

The ancient Pueblo vision of the world was inclusive. The impulse was to leave nothing out. Pueblo oral tradition necessarily embraced all levels of human experience. Otherwise, the collective knowledge and beliefs comprising ancient Pueblo culture would have been incomplete. Thus, stories about the Creation and Emergence of human beings and animals into this world continue to be retold each year for four days and four nights during the winter solstice. The *hummah-hah* stories related events from the time long ago when human beings were still able to communicate with animals and other living things.[5] But beyond these two preceding categories, the Pueblo oral tradition knew no boundaries. Accounts of the appearance of the first Europeans (Spanish) in Pueblo country or of the tragic encounters between Pueblo people and Apache raiders were no more and no less important than stories about the biggest mule deer ever taken or adulterous couples surprised in cornfields and chicken coops. Whatever happened, the ancient people instinctively sorted events and details into a loose narrative structure. Everything became a story.

TRADITIONALLY EVERYONE, FROM the youngest child to the oldest person, was expected to listen and be able to recall or tell a portion of, if only a small detail from, a narrative account or story. Thus, the remembering and the retelling were a communal process. Even if a key figure, an elder who knew much more than others, were to die unexpectedly, the system would remain intact. Through the efforts of a great many people, the community was able to piece together valuable accounts and crucial information that might otherwise have died with an individual.

Communal storytelling was a self-correcting process in which listeners were encouraged to speak up if they noted an important fact or detail omitted. The people were happy to listen to two or three different versions of the same event of the same *hummah-hah* story. Even conflicting versions of an incident were welcomed for the entertainment they provided. Defenders of each version might joke and tease one another, but seldom were there any direct confrontations. Implicit in the Pueblo oral tradition was the awareness that loyalties, grudges, and kinship must always influence the narrator's choices as she emphasizes to listeners that this is the way *she* has always heard the story told. The ancient Pueblo people sought a communal truth, not an absolute truth. For them this truth lived somewhere within the web of differing versions, disputes over minor points, and outright contradictions tangling with old feuds and village rivalries.

A dinner-table conversation recalling a deer hunt forty years ago, when the largest mule deer ever was taken, inevitably stimulates similar memories in listeners. But hunting stories were not merely after-dinner entertainment. These accounts contained information of critical importance about the behavior and migration patterns of mule deer. Hunting stories carefully described key landmarks and locations of fresh water. Thus, a deer-hunt story might also serve as a map. Lost travelers and lost piñon-nut gatherers have been saved by sighting a rock formation they recognize only because they once heard a hunting story describing this rock formation.

The importance of cliff formations and water holes does not end with hunting stories. As offspring of the Mother Earth, the ancient Pueblo people could not conceive of themselves within a specific landscape, but location, or place, nearly always plays a central role in the Pueblo oral narratives. Indeed, stories are most frequently recalled as people are passing by a specific geographical feature or the exact location where a story took place. The precise date of the incident often is less important than the place or location of the happening. "Long, long ago," "a long time ago," "not too long ago," and "recently" are usually how stories are classified in terms of time. But the places where the stories occur are precisely located, and prominent geographical details recalled, even if the landscape is well known to listeners, often because the turning point in the narrative involved a peculiarity of the special quality of a rock or tree or plant found only at that place. Thus, in the case of many of the Pueblo narratives, it is impossible to determine which came first, the incident or the geographical feature that begs to be brought alive in a story that features some unusual aspect of this location.

There is a giant sandstone boulder about a mile north of Old Laguna, on the road to Paguate. It is ten feet tall and twenty feet in circumference. When I was a child and we would pass this boulder driving to Paguate village, someone usually made reference to the story about Kochininako, Yellow Woman, and the Estrucuyo, a monstrous giant who nearly ate her. The Twin Hero Brothers saved Kochininako, who had been out hunting rabbits to take home to feed her mother and sisters. The Hero Brothers had heard her cries just in time. The Estrucuyo had cornered her in a cave too small to fit its monstrous head. Kochininako had already thrown to the Estrucuyo all her rabbits, as well as her moccasins and most of her clothing. Still the creature had not been satisfied. After killing the Estrucuyo with her bows and arrows, the Twin Hero Brothers slit open the Estrucuyo and cut out its heart. They threw the heart as far as they could.

The monster's heart landed there, beside the old trail to Paguate village, where the sandstone boulder rests now.

It may be argued that the existence of the boulder precipitated the creation of a story to explain it. But sandstone boulders and sandstone formations of strange shapes abound in the Laguna Pueblo area. Yet, most of them do not have stories. Often the crucial element in a narrative is the terrain—some specific detail of the setting.

A high, dark mesa rises dramatically from a grassy plain, fifteen miles southeast of Laguna, in an area known as Swahnee. On the grassy plain 140 years ago, my great-grandmother's uncle and his brother-in-law were grazing their herd of sheep. Because visibility on the plain extends for over twenty miles, it wasn't until the two sheepherders came near the high, dark mesa that the Apaches were able to stalk them. Using the mesa to obscure their approach, the raiders swept around from both ends of the mesa. My great-grandmother's relatives were killed, and the herd was lost. The high, dark mesa played a critical role: the mesa had compromised the safety that the openness of the plains had seemed to assure.

Pueblo and Apache alike relied upon the terrain, the very earth herself, to give them protection and aid. Human activities or needs were maneuvered to fit the existing surroundings and conditions. I imagine the last afternoon of my distant ancestors as warm and sunny for late September. They might have been traveling slowly, bringing the sheep closer to Laguna in preparation for the approach of colder weather. The grass was tall and only beginning to change from green to a yellow that matched the late afternoon sun shining off it. There might have been comfort in the warmth and the sight of the sheep fattening on good pasture that lulled my ancestors into their fatal inattention. They might have had a rifle, whereas the Apaches had only bows and arrows. But there would have been four or five Apache raiders, and the surprise attack would have canceled any advantage the rifles gave them.

Survival in any landscape comes down to making the best use of all available resources. On that particular September afternoon, the raiders made better use of the Swahnee terrain than my poor ancestors did. Thus, the high, dark mesa and the story of the two lost Laguna herders became inextricably linked. The memory of them and their story resides in part with the high, dark mesa. For as long as the mesa stands, people within the family and clan will be reminded of the story of that afternoon long ago. Thus, the continuity and accuracy of the oral narratives are reinforced by the landscape—and the Pueblo interpretation of that landscape is *maintained*.

THE MIGRATION STORY: AN INTERIOR JOURNEY

THE LAGUNA PUEBLO migration stories refer to specific places—mesas, springs, or cottonwood trees—not only locations that can be visited still, but also locations that lie directly on the state highway route linking Paguate village with Laguna village.[6] In traveling this road as a child with older Laguna people I first heard a few of the stories from that much larger body of stories linked with the Emergence and Migration.[7] It may be coincidental that Laguna people continue to follow the same route that, according to the Migration story, the ancestors followed south from the Emergence Place. It may be that the route is merely the shortest and best route for car, horse, or foot traffic between Laguna and Paguate villages. But if the stories about boulders, springs, and hills are actually remnants from a ritual that retraces the Creation and Emergence of the Laguna Pueblo people as a culture, as the people they became, then continued use of that route creates a unique relationship between the ritual-mythic world and the actual, everyday world. A journey from Paguate to Laguna down the long decline of Paguate Hill retraces the original journey from the Emergence Place, which is located slightly north of the Paguate village. Thus, the landscape between Paguate and Laguna takes on a deeper significance: the landscape resonates the spiritual, or mythic, dimension of the Pueblo world even today.

Although each Pueblo culture designates its Emergence Place, usually a small natural spring edged with mossy sandstone and full of cattails and wild watercress, it is clear the Pueblo people do not view any single location or natural springs as the one and only true Emergence Place. Each Pueblo group recounts stories connected with Creation, Emergence, and Migration, although it is believed that all human beings, with all the animals and plants, emerged at the same place and at the same time.[8]

Natural springs are crucial sources of water for all life in the high desert and plateau country. So the small spring near Paguate village is literally the source and continuance of life for the people in the area. The spring also functions on a spiritual level, recalling the original Emergence Place and linking the people and the springwater to all other people and to that moment when the Pueblo people became aware of themselves as they are even now. The Emergence was an emergence into a precise cultural identity. Thus, the Pueblo stories about the Emergence and Migration are not to be taken as literally as the anthropologists might wish. Prominent geographical features and landmarks that are mentioned in the narratives exist for ritual purposes, not because the Laguna people actually journeyed south for hundreds of years from Chaco Canyon or Mesa Verde, as the archaeologists say, or eight miles from the site of the natural springs at Paguate to the sandstone hilltop at Laguna.[9]

The eight miles, marked with boulders, mesas, springs, and river crossings, are actually a ritual circuit, or path, that marks the interior journey the Laguna people made: a journey of awareness and imagination in which they emerged from being within the earth and all-included in the earth to the culture and people they became, differentiating themselves for the first time from all that had surrounded them, always aware that interior distances cannot be reckoned in physical miles or in calendar years.

The narratives linked with prominent features of the landscape between Paguate and Laguna delineate the complexities of the relationship that human beings must maintain with the surrounding natural world if they hope to survive in this place. Thus, the journey was an interior process of the imagination, a growing awareness that being human is somehow different from all other life—animal, plant, and inanimate. Yet, we are all from the same source: awareness never deteriorated into Cartesian duality, cutting off the human from the natural world.

THE PEOPLE FOUND the opening into the Fifth World too small to allow them or any of the small animals to escape. They had sent a fly out through the small hole to tell them if it was the world the Mother Creator had promised. It was, but there was the problem of getting out. The antelope tried to butt the opening to enlarge it, but the antelope enlarged it only a little. It was necessary for the badger with her long claws to assist the antelope, and at last the opening was enlarged enough so that all the people and animals were able to emerge up into the Fifth World. The human beings could not have emerged without the aid of antelope and badger. The human beings depended upon the aid and charity of the animals. Only through interdependence could the human beings survive. Families belonged to clans, and it was by clan that the human being joined with the animal and plant world. Life on the high, arid plateau became viable when the human beings were able to imagine themselves as sisters and brothers to the badger, antelope, clay, yucca, and sun. Not until they could find a viable relationship to the terrain—the physical landscape they found themselves in—could they *emerge.* Only at the moment that the requisite balance between human and *other* was realized could the Pueblo people become a culture, a distinct group whose population and survival remained stable despite the vicissitudes of the climate and terrain.

Landscape thus has similarities with dreams. Both have the power to seize terrifying feelings and deep instincts and translate them into images—visual, aural, tactile—and into the concrete, where human beings may more readily confront and channel the terrifying instincts or powerful emotions into rituals and narratives that reassure the individual while reaffirming cherished values of the group. The identity of the individual as a part of the group and the greater Whole is strengthened, and the terror of facing the world alone is extinguished.

Even now, the people at Laguna Pueblo spend the greater portion of social occasions recounting recent incidents or events that have occurred in the Laguna area. Nearly always, the discussion will precipitate the retelling of older stories about similar incidents or other stories connected with a specific place. The stories often contain disturbing or provocative material but are nonetheless told in the presence of children and women. The effect of these interfamily or interclan exchanges is the reassurance for each person that she or he will never be separated or apart from the clan, no matter what might happen. Neither the worst blunders or disasters nor the greatest financial prosperity and joy will ever be permitted to isolate anyone from the rest of the group. In the ancient times cohesiveness was all that stood between extinction and survival, and while the individual certainly was recognized, it was always as an individual simultaneously bonded to family and clan by a complex bundle of custom and ritual. You are never the first to suffer a grave loss or profound humiliation. You are never the first, and you understand that you will probably not be the last to commit, or be victimized by, a repugnant act. Your family and clan are able to go on at length about others now passed on and others older or more experienced than you who suffered similar losses.

The wide, deep arroyo near the King's Bar (located across the reservation's borderline) has over the years claimed many vehicles. A few years ago, a Vietnam veteran's new red Volkswagen rolled backward into the arroyo while he was inside buying a six-pack of beer; the story of his loss joined the lively and large collection of stories already connected with that big arroyo. I do not know whether the Vietnam veteran was consoled when he was told the stories about the other cars claimed by the ravenous arroyo. All his savings of combat pay had gone to buy the red Volkswagen. But this man could not have felt any worse than the man who, some years before, had left his children and mother-in-law in his station wagon with the engine running. When he came out of the liquor store his station wagon was gone. He found it and its passengers upside down in the big arroyo: broken bones, cuts, and bruises, and a total wreck of the car.

The big arroyo has a wide mouth. Its existence needs no

explanation. People in the area regard the arroyo much as they might regard a living being, which has a certain character and personality. I seldom drive past that wide, deep arroyo without feeling a familiarity and even a strange affection for it, because as treacherous as it may be, the arroyo maintains a strong connection between human beings and the earth. The arroyo demands from us the caution and attention that constitute respect. It is this sort of respect the old believers have in mind when they tell us we must respect and love the earth.

Hopi Pueblo elders said that the austere and, to some eyes, barren plains and hills surrounding their mesa-top villages (in northeast Arizona) actually help to nurture the spirituality of the Hopi *way*. The Hopi elders say the Hopi people might have settled in locations far more lush, where daily life would not have been so grueling. But there on the high, silent, sandstone mesas that overlook the sandy, arid expanses stretching to all horizons, the Hopi elders say the Hopi people must "live by their prayers" if they are to survive. The Hopi way cherishes the intangible: the riches realized from interaction and interrelationships with all beings above all else. Great abundances of material things, even food, the Hopi elders believe, tend to lure human attention away from what is most valuable and important. The views of the Hopi elders are not much different from those of elders in all the pueblos.

The bare but beautiful vastness of the Hopi landscape emphasizes the visual impact of every plant, every rock, every arroyo. Nothing is overlooked or taken for granted. Each ant, each lizard, each lark is imbued with great value simply because the creature is there, simply because the creature is alive in a place where any life at all is precious. Stand on the mesa's edge at Walpi and look southwest over the bare distances toward the pale blue outlines of the San Francisco Peaks (north of Flagstaff) where the *ka'tsina* spirits reside. So little lies between you and the sky. So little lies between you and the earth. One look and you know that simply to survive is a great triumph, that every possible resource is needed, every possible ally—even the most humble insect or reptile. You realize you will be speaking with all of them if you intend to last out the year. Thus it is that the Hopi elders are grateful to the landscape for aiding them in their quest as spiritual people.

OUT UNDER THE SKY

MY EARLIEST MEMORIES are of being outside, under the sky. I remember climbing the fence when I was three years old and heading for the plaza in the center of Laguna village because other children passing by had told me there were *ka'tsinas* there dancing with pieces of wood in their mouths. A neighbor, a woman, retrieved me before I ever saw the wood-swallowing *ka'tsinas*, but from an early age I knew I wanted to be outside: outside walls and fences.

My father had wandered over all the hills and mesas around Laguna when he was a child, because the Indian School and the taunts of the other children did not sit well with him. It had been difficult in those days to be part Laguna and part white, or *amedicana*. It was still difficult when I attended the Indian School at Laguna. Our full-blooded relatives and clanspeople assured us we were theirs and that we belonged there because we had been born and reared there. But the racism of the wider world we call America had begun to make itself felt years before. My father's response was to head for the mesas and hills with his older brother, their dog, and .22 rifles. They retreated to the sandstone cliffs and juniper forests. Out in the hills they were not lonely because they had all the living creatures of the hills around them, and whatever the ambiguities of racial heritage, my father and my uncle understood what the old folks had taught them: the earth loves all of us regardless, because we are her children.

I started roaming those same mesas and hills when I was nine years old. At eleven I rode away on my horse and explored places my father and uncle could not have reached on foot. I was never afraid or lonely—though I was high in the hills, many miles from home—because I carried with me the feeling I'd acquired from listening to the old stories, that the land all around me was teeming with creatures that were related to human beings and to me. The stories had also left me with a feeling of familiarity and warmth for the mesas, hills, and boulders where the incidents or action in the stories had taken place. I felt as if I had actually been to those places, although I had only heard stories about them. Somehow the stories had given a kind of being to the mesas and hills, just as the stories had left me with the sense of having spent time with the people in the stories, though they had long since passed on.

It is remarkable to sense the presence of those long passed at the locations where their adventures took place. Spirits range without boundaries of any sort, and spirits may be called back in any number of ways. The method used in the calling also determines how the spirit manifests itself. I think a spirit may or may not choose to remain at the site of its passing or death. I think they might be in a number of places at the same time. Storytelling can procure fleeting moments to experience who they were and how life felt long ago. What I enjoyed most as a child was standing at the site of an incident recounted in one of the ancient stories that old Aunt Susie had told us as girls. What excited me was listening to her tell us an old-time story and then realizing that I was familiar with a certain mesa or cave that figured as the central location of the story she was telling. That was when the stories worked best, because then I could sit there listening and be able to visualize myself as being located *within* the story being told, within the landscape. Because the storytellers did not just tell the stories, they would in their way act them out. The storyteller would imitate voices for vast dialogues between the various figures in the story. So we sometimes say the moment is alive again within us, within our imaginations and our memory, as we listen.

Aunt Susie once told me how it had been when she was a child and her grandmother agreed to tell the children stories. The old woman would always ask the youngest child in the room to go open the door. "Go open the door," her grandmother would say. "Go open the door so our esteemed ancestors may bring us the precious gift of their stories." Two points seem clear: the spirits could be present, and the stories were valuable because they taught us how we were the people we believed we were. The myth, the web of memories and ideas that create an identity, is a part of oneself. This sense of identity was intimately linked with the surrounding terrain, to the landscape that has often played a significant role in a story or in the outcome of a conflict.

The landscape sits in the center of Pueblo belief and identity. Any narratives about the Pueblo people necessarily give a great deal of attention and detail to all aspects of a landscape. For this reason, the Pueblo people have always been extremely reluctant to relinquish their land for dams or highways. For this reason, Taos Pueblo fought from 1906 until 1973 to win back its sacred Blue Lake, which was illegally taken by the creation of Taos National Forest. For this reason, the decision in the early 1950s to begin open-pit mining of the huge uranium deposits north of Laguna, near Paguate village, has had a powerful psychological impact upon the Laguna people. Already a large body of stories has grown up around the subject of what happens to people who disturb or destroy the earth. I was a child when the mining began and the apocalyptic warning stories were being told. And I have lived long enough to begin hearing the stories that verify the earlier warnings.

All that remains of the gardens and orchards that used to grow in the sandy flats southeast of Paguate village are the stories of the lovely big peaches and apricots the people used to grow. The Jackpile Mine is an open pit that has been blasted out of the many hundreds of acres where the orchards and melon patches once grew. The Laguna people have not witnessed changes to the land without strong reactions. Descriptions of the landscape *before* the mine are as vivid as any description of the present-day destruction by the open-pit mining. By its very ugliness and by the violence it does to the land, the Jackpile Mine insures that, from now on, it, too, will be included in the vast body of narratives that makes up the history of the Laguna people and the Pueblo landscape. And the description of what that landscape looked like *before* the uranium mining began will always carry considerable impact.

LANDSCAPE AS A CHARACTER IN FICTION

WHEN I BEGAN writing I found that the plots of my short stories very often featured the presence of elements out of the landscape, elements that directly influenced the outcome of events. Nowhere is landscape more crucial to the outcome than in my short story "Storyteller." The site is southwest Alaska in the Yukon Delta National Wildlife Refuge, near the village of Bethel, on the Kuskokwim River. Tundra country. Here the winter landscape can suddenly metamorphose into a seamless, blank white so solid that pilots in aircraft without electronic instruments lose their bearings and crash their planes into the frozen tundra, believing down to be up. Here on the Alaskan tundra, in mid-February, not all the space-age fabrics, electronics, or engines can ransom human beings from the restless, shifting forces of the winter sky and winter earth.

The young Yupik Eskimo woman works out an elaborate yet subconscious plan to avenge the deaths of her parents. After months of baiting the trap, she lures the murderer onto the river's ice, where he falls through to his death. The murderer is a white man who operated the village trading post. For years the murderer has existed like a parasite, exploiting not only the fur-bearing animals and the fish, but also the Yupik people themselves. When the Yupik woman kills him, the white trader has just finished cashing in on the influx of workers who have suddenly come to the tiny village for the petroleum exploration and pipeline.

For the Yupik people, souls deserving punishment spend varying lengths of time in a place of freezing. The Yupik see the world's end coming with ice, not fire. Although the white trader possessed every possible garment, insulation, heating fuel, and gadget ever devised to protect him from the frozen tundra environment, he still dies, drowning under the freezing river ice, because the white man had not reckoned with the true power of that landscape, especially not the power that the Yupik woman understood instinctively and that she used so swiftly and efficiently. The white man had reckoned with the young woman and determined he could overpower her. But the white man failed to account for the conjunction of the landscape with the woman. The Yupik woman had never seen herself as anything but a part of that sky, that frozen river, that tundra. The river's ice and the blinding white are her accomplices, and yet the Yupik woman never for a moment misunderstands her own relationship with that landscape.

After the white trader has crashed through the river's ice, the young woman finds herself a great distance from either shore of the treacherous, frozen river. She can see nothing but the whiteness of the sky swallowing the earth. But far away in the distance, on the side of her log and tundra-sod cabin, she is able to see a spot of bright red: a bright red marker she had nailed up weeks earlier because she was intrigued by the contrast between all that white and the spot of brilliant red. The Yupik woman knows the appetite of the frozen river. She realizes that the ice and the fog, the tundra and the snow seek constantly to be reunited with the living beings that skitter across it. The Yupik woman knows that inevitably she and all things will one day lie in those depths. But the woman is young and her instinct is to live. The Yupik woman knows how to do this.

Inside the small cabin of logs and tundra sod, the old storyteller is mumbling the last story he will ever tell. It is the story of the hunter stalking a giant polar bear the color of blue glacier ice. It is a story that the old storyteller has been telling since the young Yupik woman began to arrange the white trader's death:

> *A sudden storm develops. The hunter finds himself on an ice floe offshore. Visibility is zero, and the scream of the wind blots out all sound. Quickly the hunter realizes he is being stalked, hunted by all the forces, by all the elements of the sky and earth around him. When at last the hunter's own*

muscles spasm and cause the jade knife to fall and shatter the ice, the hunter's death in the embrace of the giant, ice blue bear is the foretelling of the world's end.

When humans have blasted and burned the last bit of life from the earth, an immeasurable freezing will descend with a darkness that obliterates the sun.

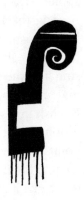

Language and Literature from a Pueblo Indian Perspective

WHERE I COME from, the words most highly valued are those spoken from the heart, unpremeditated and unrehearsed. Among the Pueblo people, a written speech or statement is highly suspect because the true feelings of the speaker remain hidden as she reads words that are detached from the occasion and the audience. I have intentionally not written a formal paper because I want you to *hear* and to experience English in a structure that follows patterns from the oral tradition. For those of you accustomed to being taken from point A to point B to point C, this presentation may be somewhat difficult to follow. Pueblo expression resembles something like a spider's web—with many little threads radiating from the center, crisscrossing one another. As with the web, the structure emerges as it is made, and you must simply listen and trust, as the Pueblo people do, that meaning will be made.

My task is a formidable one: I ask you to set aside a number of basic approaches that you have been using and probably will continue to use, and, instead, to approach language from the Pueblo perspective, one that embraces the whole of creation and the whole of history and time.

What changes would Pueblo writers make to English as a language for literature? I have some examples of stories in English that I will use to address this question. At the same time, I would like to explain the importance of storytelling and how it relates to a Pueblo theory of language.

So I will begin, appropriately enough, with the Pueblo Creation story, an all-inclusive story of how life began. In this story, Tse'itsi'nako, Thought Woman, by thinking of her sisters, and together with her sisters, thought of everything that is. In this way, the world was created. Everything in this world was a part of the original Creation; the people at home understood that far away there were other human beings, also a part of this world. The Creation story even includes a prophecy that describes the origin of European and African peoples and also refers to Asians.

This story, I think, suggests something about why the Pueblo people are more concerned with story and communication and less concerned with a particular language. There are at least six, possibly seven, distinct languages among the twenty pueblos of the southwestern United States, for example, Zuñi and Hopi. And from mesa to mesa there are subtle differences in language. But the particular language being spoken isn't as important as what a speaker is trying to say, and this emphasis on the story itself stems, I believe, from a view of narrative particular to the Pueblo and other Native American peoples—that is, that language *is* story.

I will try to clarify this statement. At Laguna Pueblo, for example, many individual words have their own stories. So when one is telling a story and one is using words to tell the story, each word that one is speaking has a story of its own, too. Often the speakers, or tellers, will go into these word stories, creating an elaborate structure of stories within stories. This structure, which becomes very apparent in the actual telling of a story, informs contemporary Pueblo writing and storytelling as well as the traditional narratives. This perspective on narrative—of story within story, the idea that one story is only the beginning of many stories and the sense that stories never truly end—represents an important contribution of Native American cultures to the English language.

Many people think of storytelling as something that is done at bedtime, that it is something done for small children. But when I use the term *storytelling,* I'm talking about something much bigger than that. I'm talking about something that comes out of an experience and an understanding of that original view of Creation—that we are all part of a whole; we do not differentiate or fragment stories and experiences. In the beginning, Tse'itsi'nako, Thought Woman, thought of all things, and all of these things are held together as one holds many things together in a single thought.

So in the telling (and you will hear a few of the dimensions of this telling), first of all, as mentioned earlier, the storytelling always includes the audience, the listeners. In fact, a great deal of the story is believed to be inside the listener; the storyteller's role is to draw the story out of the listeners. The storytelling continues from generation to generation.

Basically, the origin story constructs our identity—with this story, we know who we are. We are the Lagunas. This is where we come from. We came this way. We came by this place. And so from the time we are very young, we hear these stories, so that when we go out into the world, when one asks who we are or where we are from, we immediately know: we are the people who came from the north. We are the people of these stories.

In the Creation story, Antelope says that he will help knock a hole in the Earth so that the people can come up, out into the next world. Antelope tries and tries; he uses his hooves but is unable to break through. It is then that Badger says, "Let me help you." And Badger very patiently uses his claws and digs a way through, bringing the people into the world. When the Badger clan people think of themselves, or when the Antelope people think of themselves, it is as people who are of *this* story, and this is *our* place, and we fit into the very beginning when the people first came, before we began our journey south.

Within the clans there are stories that identify the clan. One moves, then, from the idea of one's identity as a tribal person into clan identity, then to one's identity as a member of an extended family. And it is the notion of extended family that has produced a kind of story that some distinguish from other Pueblo stories, though Pueblo people do not. Anthropologists and ethnologists have, for a long time, differentiated the types of stories the Pueblos tell. They tended to elevate the old, sacred, and traditional stories and to brush aside family stories, the family's account of itself. But in Pueblo culture, these family stories are given equal recognition. There is no definite, preset pattern for the way one will hear the stories of one's own family, but it is a very critical part of one's childhood, and the storytelling continues throughout one's life. One will hear stories of importance to the family—sometimes wonderful stories—stories about the time a maternal uncle got the biggest deer that was ever seen and brought it back from the mountains. And so an individual's identity will extend from the identity constructed around the family—"I am from the family of my uncle who brought in this wonderful deer, and it was a wonderful hunt."

Family accounts include negative stories, too; perhaps an uncle did something unacceptable. It is very important that one keep track of all these stories—both positive and not so positive—about one's own family and other families. Because even when there is no way around it—old Uncle Pete *did* do a terrible thing—by knowing the stories that originate in other families, one is able to deal with terrible sorts of things that might happen within one's own family. If a member of the family does something that cannot be excused, one always knows stories about similarly inexcusable things done by a member of another family. But this knowledge is not communicated for malicious reasons. It is very important to understand this. Keeping track of all the stories within the community gives us all a certain distance, a useful perspective, that brings incidents down to a level we can deal with. If others have done it before, it cannot be so terrible. If others have endured, so can we.

The stories are always bringing us together, keeping this whole together, keeping this family together, keeping this clan together. "Don't go away, don't isolate yourself, but come here, because we have all had these kinds of experiences." And so there is this constant pulling together to resist the tendency to run or hide or separate oneself during a traumatic emotional experience. This separation not only endangers the group but the individual as well—one does not recover by oneself.

Because storytelling lies at the heart of Pueblo culture, it is absurd to attempt to fix the stories in time. "When did they tell the stories?" or "What time of day does the storytelling take place?"—these questions are nonsensical from a Pueblo perspective, because our storytelling goes on constantly: as some old grandmother puts on the shoes of a child and tells her the story of a little girl who didn't wear her shoes, for instance, or someone comes into the house for coffee to talk with a teenage boy who has just been in a lot of trouble, to reassure him that someone else's son has been in that kind of trouble, too. Storytelling is an ongoing process, working on many different levels.

Here's one story that is often told at a time of individual crisis (and I want to remind you that we make no distinctions between types of story—historical, sacred, plain gossip—because these distinctions are not useful when discussing the Pueblo *experience* of language). There was a young man who, when he came back from the war in Vietnam, had saved up his army pay and bought a beautiful red Volkswagen. He was very proud of it. One night he drove up to a place called the King's Bar, right across the reservation line. The bar is notorious for many reasons, particularly for the deep arroyo located behind it. The young man ran in to pick up a cold six-pack, but he forgot to put on his emergency brake. And his little red Volkswagen rolled back into the arroyo and was all smashed up. He felt very bad about it, but within a few days everybody had come to him with stories about other people who had lost cars and family members to that arroyo, for instance, George Day's station wagon, with his mother-in-law and kids inside. So everybody was saying, "Well, at least your mother-in-law and kids weren't in the car when it rolled in," and one can't argue with that kind of story. The story of the young man and his smashed-up Volkswagen was now joined with all the other stories of cars that fell into that arroyo.

Now I want to tell you a very beautiful little story. It is a very old story that is sometimes told to people who suffer great family or personal loss. This story was told by my Aunt Susie. She is one of the first generation of people at Laguna who began experimenting with English—who began working to make English speak for us, that is, to speak from the heart. (I come from a family intent on getting the stories told.) As you read the story, I think you will hear that. And here and there, I think, you will also hear the influence of the Indian school at Carlisle, Pennsylvania, where my Aunt Susie was sent (like being sent to prison) for six years.

This scene is set partly in Acoma, partly in Laguna. Waithea was a little girl living in Acoma and one day she said, "Mother, I would like to have some *yashtoah* to eat." *Yashtoah* is the hardened crust of corn mush that curls up. *Yashtoah* literally means "curled up." She said, "I would like to have some *yashtoah*," and her mother said, "My dear little girl, I can't make you any *yashtoah* because we haven't any wood, but if you will go down off the mesa, down below, and pick up some pieces of wood and bring them home, I will make you some *yashtoah*." So Waithea was glad and ran down the precipitous cliff of Acoma mesa. Down below, just as her mother had told her, there were pieces of wood, some curled, some crooked in shape, that she was to pick up and take home. She found just such wood as these.

She brought them home in a little wicker basket. First she called to her mother as she got home, "*Nayah, deeni!* Mother, upstairs!" The Pueblo people always called "upstairs" because long ago their homes were two, three stories, and they entered from the top. She said, "*Deeni! Upstairs!*" and her mother came. The little girl said, "I have brought the wood you wanted me to bring." And she opened her little wicker basket to lay out the pieces of wood, but here they were snakes. They were snakes instead of the crooked sticks of wood. And her mother said, "Oh my dear child, you have brought snakes instead!" She said, "Go take them back and put them back just where you got them." And the little girl ran down the mesa again, down below to the flats. And she put those snakes back just where she got them. They were snakes instead, and she was very hurt about this, and so she said, "I'm not going home. I'm going to Kawaik, the beautiful lake place Kawaik, and drown myself in that lake, *byn'yah'nah* [the 'west lake']. I will go there and drown myself."

So she started off, and as she passed by the Enchanted Mesa near Acoma, she met an old man, very aged, and he saw her running, and he said, "My dear child, where are you going?" "I'm going to Kawaik and jump into the lake there."

"Why?" "Well, because," she said, "my mother didn't want to make any *yashtoah* for me." The old man said, "Oh, no! You must not go, my child. Come with me and I will take you home." He tried to catch her, but she was very light and skipped along. And every time he would try to grab her she would skip faster away from him.

The old man was coming home with some wood strapped to his back and tied with yucca. He just let that strap go and let the wood drop. He went as fast as he could up the cliff to the little girl's home. When he got to the place where she lived, he called to her mother. "*Deeni!*" "Come on up!" And he said, "I can't. I just came to bring you a message. Your little daughter is running away. She is going to Kawaik to drown herself in the lake there." "Oh my dear little girl!" the mother said. So she busied herself with making the *yashtoah* her little girl liked so much. Corn mush curled at the top. (She must have found enough wood to boil the corn meal and make the *yashtoah*.)

While the mush was cooling off, she got the little girl's

clothing, her *manta* dress and buckskin moccasins and all her other garments, and put them in a bundle—probably a yucca bag. And she started down as fast as she could on the east side of Acoma. (There used to be a trail there, you know. It's gone now, but it was accessible in those days.) She saw her daughter way at a distance and she kept calling: "Stsamaku! My daughter! Come back! I've got your *yashtoah* for you." But the little girl would not turn. She kept on ahead and she cried: "My mother, my mother, she didn't want me to have any *yashtoah*. So now I'm going to Kawaik and drown myself." Her mother heard her cry and said, "My little daughter, come back here!" "No," and she kept a distance away from her. And they came nearer and nearer to the lake. And she could see her daughter now, very plain. "Come back, my daughter! I have your *yashtoah*." But no, she kept on, and finally she reached the lake and she stood on the edge.

She had tied a little feather in her hair, which is traditional (in death they tie this feather on the head). She carried a feather, the little girl did, and she tied it in her hair with a piece of string; right on top of her head she put the feather. Just as her mother was about to reach her, she jumped into the lake. The little feather was whirling around and around in the depths below. Of course the mother was very sad. She went, grieved, back to Acoma and climbed her mesa home. She stood on the edge of the mesa and scattered her daughter's clothing, the little moccasins, the *yashtoah*. She scattered them to the east, to the west, to the north, to the south. And the pieces of clothing and the moccasins and *yashtoah* all turned into butterflies. And today they say that Acoma has more beautiful butterflies: red ones, white ones, blue ones, yellow ones. They came from this little girl's clothing.

Now this is a story anthropologists would consider very

old. The version I have given you is just as Aunt Susie tells it. You can occasionally hear some English she picked up at Carlisle—words like *precipitous.* You will also notice that there is a great deal of repetition, and a little reminder about *yashtoah* and how it is made. There is a remark about the cliff trail at Acoma—that it was once there but is there no longer. This story may be told at a time of sadness or loss, but within this story many other elements are brought together. Things are not separated out and categorized; all things are brought together, so that the reminder about the *yashtoah* is valuable information that is repeated—a recipe, if you will. The information about the old trail at Acoma reveals that stories are, in a sense, maps, since even to this day there is little information or material about trails that is passed around with writing. In the structure of this story the repetitions are, of course, designed to help you remember. It is repeated again and again, and then it moves on.

There are a great many parallels between Pueblo experiences and those of African and Caribbean peoples—one is that we have all had the conqueror's language imposed on us. But our experience with English has been somewhat different in that the Bureau of Indian Affairs schools were not interested in teaching us the canon of Western classics. For instance, we never heard of Shakespeare. We were given Dick and Jane, and I can remember reading that the robins were heading south for the winter. It took me a long time to figure out what was going on. I worried for quite a while about our robins in Laguna because they didn't leave in the winter, until I finally realized that all the big textbook companies are up in Boston and *their* robins do go south in the winter. But in a way, this dreadful formal education freed us by encouraging us to maintain our narratives. Whatever literature we were exposed to at school (which was damn little), at home the storytelling, the special regard for telling and bringing together through the telling, was going on constantly.

And as the old people say, "If you can remember the stories, you will be all right. Just remember the stories." When I returned to Laguna Pueblo after attending college, I wondered how the storytelling was continuing (anthropologists say that Laguna Pueblo is one of the more acculturated pueblos), so I visited an English class at Laguna-Acoma High School. I knew the students had cassette tape recorders in their lockers and stereos at home, and that they listened to Kiss and Led Zeppelin and were well informed about culture in general. I had with me an anthology of short stories by Native American writers, *The Man to Send Rain Clouds*. One story in the book is about the killing of a state policeman in New Mexico by three Acoma Pueblo men in the early 1950s. I asked the students how many had heard this story and steeled myself for the possibility that the anthropologists were right, that the old traditions were indeed dying out and the students would be ignorant of the story. But instead, all but one or two raised their hands—they had heard the story, just as I had heard it when I was young, some in English, some in Laguna.

One of the other advantages that we Pueblos have enjoyed is that we have always been able to stay with the land. Our stories cannot be separated from their geographical locations, from actual physical places on the land. We were not relocated like so many Native American groups who were torn away from their ancestral land. And our stories are so much a part of these places that it is almost impossible for future generations to lose them—there is a story connected with every place, every object in the landscape.

Dennis Brutus has talked about the "yet unborn" as well as "those from the past," and how we are still *all* in *this* place, and language—the storytelling—is our way of passing through or being with them, of being together again. When Aunt Susie told her stories, she would tell a younger child to go open the door so that our esteemed predecessors might bring their gifts to us. "They are out there," Aunt Susie would say. "Let them come in. They're here, they're here with us *within* the stories."

A few years ago, when Aunt Susie was 106, I paid her a visit, and while I was there she said, "Well, I'll be leaving here soon. I think I'll be leaving here next week, and I will be going over to the Cliff House." She said, "It's going to be real good to get back over there." I was listening, and I was thinking that she must be talking about her house at Paguate village, just north of Laguna. And she went on, "Well, my mother's sister [and she gave her Indian name] will be there. She has been living there. She will be there and we will be over there, and I will get a chance to write down these stories I've been telling you." Now you must understand, of course, that Aunt Susie's mother's sister, a great storyteller herself, has long since passed over into the land of the dead. But then I realized, too, that Aunt Susie wasn't talking about death the way most of us do. She was talking about "going over" as a journey, a journey that perhaps we can only begin to understand through an appreciation for the boundless capacity of language that, through storytelling, brings us together, despite great distances between cultures, despite great distances in time.

Yellow Woman and a Beauty of the Spirit

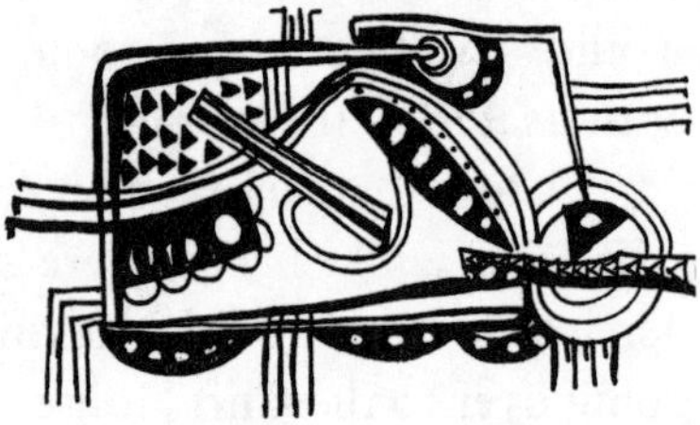

FROM THE TIME I was a small child, I was aware that I was different. I looked different from my playmates. My two sisters looked different too. We didn't look quite like the other Laguna Pueblo children, but we didn't look quite white either. In the 1880s, my great-grandfather had followed his older brother west from Ohio to the New Mexico Territory to survey the land for the U.S. government. The two Marmon brothers came to the Laguna Pueblo reservation because they had an Ohio cousin who already lived there. The Ohio cousin was involved in sending Indian children thousands of miles away from their families to the War Department's big Indian boarding school in Carlisle, Pennsylvania. Both brothers married full-blood Laguna Pueblo women. My great-grandfather had first married my great-grandmother's older sister, but she died in childbirth and left two small children. My great-grandmother was fifteen or twenty years younger than my great-grandfather. She had attended Carlisle Indian School and spoke and wrote English beautifully.

I called her Grandma A'mooh because that's what I heard her say whenever she saw me. *A'mooh* means "granddaughter" in the Laguna language. I remember this word because her love and her acceptance of me as a small child were so important. I had sensed immediately that something about my appearance was not acceptable to some people, white and Indian. But I did not see any signs of that strain or anxiety in the face of my beloved Grandma A'mooh.

Younger people, people my parents' age, seemed to look at the world in a more modern way. The modern way included racism. My physical appearance seemed not to matter to the old-time people. They looked at the world very differently; a person's appearance and possessions did not matter nearly as much as a person's behavior. For them, a person's value lies in how that person interacts with other people, how that person behaves toward the animals and the earth. That is what matters most to the old-time people. The Pueblo people believed this long before the Puritans arrived with their notions of sin and damnation, and racism. The old-time beliefs persist today; thus I will refer to the old-time people in the present tense as well as the past. Many worlds may coexist here.

I SPENT A great deal of time with my great-grandmother. Her house was next to our house, and I used to wake up at dawn, hours before my parents or younger sisters, and I'd go wait on the porch swing or on the back steps by her kitchen door. She got up at dawn, but she was more than eighty years old, so she needed a little while to get dressed and to get the fire going in the cookstove. I had been carefully instructed by my parents not to bother her and to behave, and to try to help her any way I could. I always loved the early mornings when the air was so cool with a hint of rain smell in the breeze. In the dry New Mexico air, the least hint of dampness smells sweet.

My great-grandmother's yard was planted with lilac bushes and iris; there were four o'clocks, cosmos, morning glories, and hollyhocks, and old-fashioned rosebushes that I helped her water. If the garden hose got stuck on one of the big rocks that lined the path in the yard, I ran and pulled it free. That's what I came to do early every morning: to help Grandma water the plants before the heat of the day arrived.

Grandma A'mooh would tell about the old days, family stories about relatives who had been killed by Apache raiders who stole the sheep our relatives had been herding near Swahnee. Sometimes she read Bible stories that we kids liked because of the illustrations of Jonah in the mouth of a whale and Daniel surrounded by lions. Grandma A'mooh would send me home when she took her nap, but when the sun got low and the afternoon began to cool off, I would be back on the porch swing, waiting for her to come out to water the plants and to haul in firewood for the evening. When Grandma was eighty-five, she still chopped her own kindling. She used to let me carry in the coal bucket for her, but she would not allow me to use the ax. I carried armloads of kindling too, and I learned to be proud of my strength.

I was allowed to listen quietly when Aunt Susie or Aunt Alice came to visit Grandma. When I got old enough to cross the road alone, I went and visited them almost daily. They were vigorous women who valued books and writing. They were usually busy chopping wood or cooking but never hesitated to take time to answer my questions. Best of all they told me the *hummah-hah* stories, about an earlier time when animals and humans shared a common language. In the old days, the Pueblo people had educated their children in this manner; adults took time out to talk to and teach young people. Everyone was a teacher, and every activity had the potential to teach the child.

But as soon as I started kindergarten at the Bureau of Indian Affairs day school, I began to learn more about the differences between the Laguna Pueblo world and the outside world. It was at school that I learned just how different I looked from my classmates. Sometimes tourists driving past on Route 66 would stop by Laguna Day School at recess time to take photographs of us kids. One day, when I was in the first grade, we all crowded around the smiling white tourists, who peered at our faces. We all wanted to be in the picture because afterward the tourists sometimes gave us each a penny. Just as we were all posed and ready to have our picture taken, the tourist man looked at me. "Not you," he said and motioned for me to step away from my classmates. I felt so embarrassed that I wanted to disappear. My classmates were puzzled by the tourists' behavior, but I knew the tourists didn't want me in their snapshot because I looked different, because I was part white.

IN THE VIEW of the old-time people, we are all sisters and brothers because the Mother Creator made all of us—all colors and all sizes. We are sisters and brothers, clanspeople of all the living beings around us. The plants, the birds, fish, clouds, water, even the clay—they all are related to us. The old-time people believe that all things, even rocks and water, have spirit and being. They understood that all things want only to continue being as they are; they need only to be left as they are. Thus the old folks used to tell us kids not to disturb the earth unnecessarily. All things as they were created exist already in harmony with one another as long as we do not disturb them.

As the old story tells us, Tse'itsi'nako, Thought Woman, the Spider, thought of her three sisters, and as she thought of them, they came into being. Together with Thought Woman, they thought of the sun and the stars and the moon. The Mother Creators imagined the earth and the oceans, the animals and the people, and the *ka'tsina* spirits that reside in the mountains. The Mother Creators imagined all the plants that flower and the trees that bear fruit. As Thought Woman and her sisters thought of it, the whole universe came into being. In this universe, there is no absolute good or absolute bad; there are only balances and harmonies that ebb and flow. Some years the desert receives abundant rain, other years there is too little rain, and sometimes there is so much rain that floods cause destruction. But rain itself is neither innocent nor guilty. The rain is simply itself.

My great-grandmother was dark and handsome. Her expression in photographs is one of confidence and strength. I do not know if white people then or now would consider her beautiful. I do not know if the old-time Laguna Pueblo people considered her beautiful or if the old-time people even thought in those terms. To the Pueblo way of thinking, the act of comparing one living being with another was silly, because each being or thing is unique and therefore incomparably valuable because it is the only one of its kind. The old-time people thought it was crazy to attach such importance to a person's appearance. I understood very early that there were two distinct ways of interpreting the world. There was the white people's way and there was the Laguna way. In the Laguna way, it was bad manners to make comparisons that might hurt another person's feelings.

In everyday Pueblo life, not much attention was paid to one's physical appearance or clothing. Ceremonial clothing was quite elaborate but was used only for the sacred dances. The traditional Pueblo societies were communal and strictly egalitarian, which means that no matter how well or how poorly one might have dressed, there was no social ladder to fall from. All food and other resources were strictly shared so that no one person or group had more than another. I mention social status because it seems to me that most of the definitions of beauty in contemporary Western culture are really codes for determining social status. People no longer hide their face-lifts and they discuss their liposuctions because the point of the procedures isn't just cosmetic, it is social. It says to the world, "I have enough spare cash that I can afford surgery for cosmetic purposes."

In the old-time Pueblo world, beauty was manifested in behavior and in one's relationships with other living beings. Beauty was as much a feeling of harmony as it was a visual, aural, or sensual effect. The whole person had to be beautiful, not just the face or the body; faces and bodies could not be separated from hearts and souls. Health was foremost in achieving this sense of well-being and harmony; in the old-time Pueblo world, a person who did not look healthy inspired feelings of worry and anxiety, not feelings of well-being. A healthy person, of course, is in harmony with the world around her; she is at peace with herself too. Thus an unhappy person or spiteful person would not be considered beautiful.

In the old days, strong, sturdy women were most admired. One of my most vivid preschool memories is of the crew of Laguna women, in their forties and fifties, who came to cover our house with adobe plaster. They handled the ladders with great ease, and while two women ground the adobe mud on stones and added straw, another woman loaded the hod with mud and passed it up to the two women on ladders, who were smoothing the plaster on the wall with their hands. Since women owned the houses, they did the plastering. At Laguna, men did the basket making and the weaving of fine textiles; men helped a great deal with the child care too. Because the Creator is female, there is no stigma on being female; gender is not used to control behavior. No job was a man's job or a woman's job; the most able person did the work.

My Grandma Lily had been a Ford Model A mechanic when she was a teenager. I remember when I was young, she was always fixing broken lamps and appliances. She was small and wiry, but she could lift her weight in rolled roofing or boxes of nails. When she was seventy-five, she was still repairing washing machines in my uncle's coin-operated laundry.

The old-time people paid no attention to birthdays. When a person was ready to do something, she did it. When she no longer was able, she stopped. Thus the traditional Pueblo people did not worry about aging or about looking old because there were no social boundaries drawn by the passage of years. It was not remarkable for young men to marry women as old as their mothers. I never heard anyone talk about "women's work" until after I left Laguna for college. Work was there to be done by any able-bodied person who wanted to do it. At the same time, in the old-time Pueblo world, identity was acknowledged to be always in a flux; in the old stories, one minute Spider Woman is a little spider under a yucca plant, and the next instant she is a sprightly grandmother walking down the road.

When I was growing up, there was a young man from a nearby village who wore nail polish and women's blouses and permed his hair. People paid little attention to his appearance; he was always part of a group of other young men from his village. No one ever made fun of him. Pueblo communities were and still are very interdependent, but they also have to be tolerant of individual eccentricities because survival of the group means everyone has to cooperate.

In the old Pueblo world, differences were celebrated as signs of the Mother Creator's grace. Persons born with exceptional physical or sexual differences were highly respected and honored because their physical differences gave them special positions as mediators between this world and the spirit world. The great Navajo medicine man of the 1920s, the Crawler, had a hunchback and could not walk upright, but he was able to heal even the most difficult cases.

Before the arrival of Christian missionaries, a man could dress as a woman and work with the women and even marry a man without any fanfare. Likewise, a woman was free to dress like a man, to hunt and go to war with the men, and to marry a woman. In the old Pueblo worldview, we are all a mixture of male and female, and this sexual identity is changing constantly. Sexual inhibition did not begin until the Christian missionaries arrived. For the old-time people, marriage was about teamwork and social relationships, not about sexual excitement. In the days before the Puritans came, marriage did not mean an end to sex with people other than your spouse. Women were just as likely as men to have a *si'ash,* or lover.

New life was so precious that pregnancy was always appropriate, and pregnancy before marriage was celebrated as a good sign. Since the children belonged to the mother and her clan, and women owned and bequeathed the houses and farmland, the exact determination of paternity wasn't critical. Although fertility was prized, infertility was no problem because mothers with unplanned pregnancies gave their babies to childless couples within the clan in open adoption arrangements. Children called their mother's sisters "mother" as well, and a child became attached to a number of parent figures.

In the sacred kiva ceremonies, men mask and dress as women to pay homage and to be possessed by the female energies of the spirit beings. Because differences in physical appearance were so highly valued, surgery to change one's face and body to resemble a model's face and body would be unimaginable. To be different, to be unique was blessed and was best of all.

The traditional clothing of Pueblo women emphasized a woman's sturdiness. Buckskin leggings wrapped around the legs protected her from scratches and injuries while she worked. The more layers of buckskin, the better. All those layers gave her legs the appearance of strength, like sturdy tree trunks. To demonstrate sisterhood and brotherhood with the plants and animals, the old-time people make masks and costumes that transform the human figures of the dancers into the animal beings they portray. Dancers paint their exposed skin; their postures and motions are adapted from their observations. But the motions are stylized. The observer sees not an actual eagle or actual deer dancing, but witnesses a human being, a dancer, gradually changing into a woman/buffalo or a man/deer. Every impulse is to reaffirm the urgent relationships that human beings have with the plant and animal world.

In the high desert plateau country, all vegetation, even weeds and thorns, becomes special, and all life is precious and beautiful because without the plants, the insects, and the animals, human beings living here cannot survive. Perhaps human beings long ago noticed the devastating impact human activity can have on the plants and animals; maybe this is why tribal cultures devised the stories about humans and animals intermarrying, and the clans that bind humans to animals and plants through a whole complex of duties.

We children were always warned not to harm frogs or toads, the beloved children of the rain clouds, because terrible floods would occur. I remember in the summer the old folks used to stick big bolls of cotton on the outside of their screen doors as bait to keep the flies from going in the house when the door was opened. The old folks staunchly resisted the killing of flies because once, long, long ago, when human beings were in a great deal of trouble, a Green Bottle Fly carried the desperate messages of human beings to the Mother Creator in the Fourth World, below this one. Human beings had outraged the Mother Creator by neglecting the Mother Corn altar while they dabbled with sorcery and magic. The Mother Creator disappeared, and with her disappeared the rain clouds, and the plants and the animals too. The people began to starve, and they had no way of reaching the Mother Creator down below. Green Bottle Fly took the message to the Mother Creator, and the people were saved. To show their gratitude, the old folks refused to kill any flies.

THE OLD STORIES demonstrate the interrelationships that the Pueblo people have maintained with their plant and animal clanspeople. Kochininako, Yellow Woman, represents all women in the old stories. Her deeds span the spectrum of human behavior and are mostly heroic acts, though in at least one story, she chooses to join the secret Destroyer Clan, which worships destruction and death. Because Laguna Pueblo cosmology features a female Creator, the status of women is equal with the status of men, and women appear as often as men in the old stories as hero figures. Yellow Woman is my favorite because she dares to cross traditional boundaries of ordinary behavior during times of crisis in order to save the Pueblo; her power lies in her courage and in her uninhibited sexuality, which the old-time Pueblo stories celebrate again and again because fertility was so highly valued.

The old stories always say that Yellow Woman was beautiful, but remember that the old-time people were not so much thinking about physical appearances. In each story, the beauty that Yellow Woman possesses is the beauty of her passion, her daring, and her sheer strength to act when catastrophe is imminent.

In one story, the people are suffering during a great drought and accompanying famine. Each day, Kochininako has to walk farther and farther from the village to find fresh water for her husband and children. One day she travels far, far to the east, to the plains, and she finally locates a freshwater spring. But when she reaches the pool, the water is churning violently as if something large had just gotten out of the pool. Kochininako does not want to see what huge creature had been at the pool, but just as she fills her water jar and turns to hurry away, a strong, sexy man in buffalo-skin leggings appears by the pool. Little drops of water glisten on his chest. She cannot help but look at him because he is so strong and so good to look at. Able to transform himself from human to buffalo in the wink of an eye, Buffalo Man gallops away with her on his back. Kochininako falls in love with Buffalo Man, and because of this liaison, the Buffalo People agree to give their bodies to the hunters to feed the starving Pueblo. Thus Kochininako's fearless sensuality results in the salvation of the people of her village, who are saved by the meat the Buffalo People "give" to them.

My father taught me and my sisters to shoot .22 rifles when we were seven; I went hunting with my father when I was eight, and I killed my first mule deer buck when I was thirteen. The Kochininako stories were always my favorite because Yellow Woman had so many adventures. In one story, as she hunts rabbits to feed her family, a giant monster pursues her, but she has the courage and presence of mind to outwit it.

In another story, Kochininako has a fling with Whirlwind Man and returns to her husband ten months later with twin baby boys. The twin boys grow up to be great heroes of the people. Once again, Kochininako's vibrant sexuality benefits her people.

The stories about Kochininako made me aware that sometimes an individual must act despite disapproval, or concern for appearances or what others may say. From Yellow Woman's adventures, I learned to be comfortable with my differences. I even imagined that Yellow Woman had yellow skin, brown hair, and green eyes like mine, although her name does not refer to her color, but rather to the ritual color of the east.

There have been many other moments like the one with the camera-toting tourist in the schoolyard. But the old-time people always say, remember the stories, the stories will help you be strong. So all these years I have depended on Kochininako and the stories of her adventures.

Kochininako is beautiful because she has the courage to act in times of great peril, and her triumph is achieved by her sensuality, not through violence and destruction. For these qualities of the spirit, Yellow Woman and all women are beautiful.

America's Debt to the Indian Nations: Atoning for a Sordid Past

UNTIL INDIAN ACTIVISTS occupied Alcatraz Island, marched across the country on the Trail of Broken Treaties, and occupied the Bureau of Indian Affairs Building in Washington, the general public was content to think the Indian nations had gone out with the buffalo. But the occupation and siege at Wounded Knee in 1973 forced America to acknowledge shameful chapters in American history that had been conveniently whitewashed for so long. Unfortunately, the history lessons supplied in 1973 by the media were often simplistic and inaccurate, and they failed to report the validity of Indian claims of treaty violations and the legitimacy of other Indian grievances. The old Hollywood stereotypes of the hostile Indian uprisings were generally reinforced.

Eight years after the siege of Wounded Knee, the U.S. Commission on Civil Rights has issued a report entitled "Indian Tribes: A Continuing Quest for Survival." Although the report is long overdue, it is a landmark for two reasons: it was compiled and written largely by a staff of American Indian lawyers and Indian legal specialists who advance a unique perspective of American history and jurisprudence, and it provides the general public with detailed information that documents the history of Indian tribes and the American legal system. The basic findings—that "civil rights violations are prompted by public ignorance of Indian rights and by the failure of appropriate parties to respond promptly to any infringement of Indian rights"—will surprise no one. But the report does not hesitate to identify the "appropriate parties" or to document the deplorable tactics that federal and state governments have used to plunder Indian land, water, and energy resources.

Resulting from nearly a decade of hearings and study, the report, among other recommendations, urges Congress to recognize Indian tribes on the same basis as it recognizes states and their subdivisions for distribution of federal funds, recommends a joint congressional oversight committee on Indian affairs, and asks for "impact statements" when contemplated federal action might affect Indian rights. The Civil Rights Commission included no details, however, of what new legislation might be required, nor did it offer many specifics on changes in such matters as federal funding.

But by detailing the long history of the Indian nations' principles of international law in the fourteenth century to pending land-claims lawsuits in the 1980s, the Civil Rights Commission takes an important first step in wiping out public ignorance of Indian rights. Any questions about the unique legal status of American Indian tribes as sovereign nations or about the legal basis for Indian treaty rights and claims are answered in this document. The report addresses many of the topics most controversial to non-Indians: Indian fishing rights in the Pacific Northwest, Indian land claims on the East Coast, and the legal status of Indian tribes and their members vis-à-vis federal and state jurisdictions.

If you've ever wondered, "What right do those Washington and Oregon Indians have to 50 percent of the salmon and steelhead runs?" or, "What makes those Indians think they own all of Maine and half of Massachusetts?" then read this report. Arthur S. Flemming, chairman of the Civil Rights Commission, has observed, "There are a great many adults who do not have any understanding of the treaties, of tribal government and the implications of it . . . and they are reacting from a position of no knowledge." This report should be required reading in high school history classes, although the report notes that a basic understanding of Indian rights is lacking even in law-school curricula: "An entire volume of the U.S. Code is devoted to Indian Law. . . . Yet until the past decade, any treatment of Indian law in law schools was a rare exception."

One of the more original and controversial views to emerge from this document is that greed, not racism per se, accounts for the apparent anti-Indian backlash: "The non-Indian interests, both governmental and private, that have been unfairly profiting at Indian expense have found their individual advantages disrupted by Indian legal and political victories and have organized to recapture their preferential position," the report states. The majority of Americans are not necessarily "anti-Indian," but profiteers know how to manipulate the ignorance of the American public and the racism that is generated, not as an end in itself, but as a means to ensure continued profiteering by special interests at the expense of Indian tribes.

As the report clearly indicates, the stakes are high: Indian water rights to the Colorado, Rio Grande, San Juan, Gila, and Salt Rivers will have far-reaching effects on the growth and quality of life in Los Angeles, Phoenix, Tucson, and El Paso. Indian tribes control 3 percent of the total national oil and gas reserves and 7 to 13 percent of U.S. coal deposits. Indian tribes control a large number of extensive uranium deposits. In Washington and Oregon, enforcement of treaty provisions governing salmon and steelhead fishing rights of the Puyallup, Nisqually, Yakima, and other northwestern tribes involves millions of dollars each season. Land-claim lawsuits filed in 1975 by the Passamaquoddy and Penobscot tribes cast a cloud over the legal title to more than 10.5 million acres of land in the state of Maine. Other East Coast states face similar lawsuits. Thus, in the decades to come, it is imperative that the American public have a basic understanding of the history and legal status of Indian tribes.

From the beginning, the European governments viewed the Indian tribes of the Western Hemisphere as sovereign nations, and international law and protocol dictated that all dealings with the Indian nations (even as conquered sovereign nations) be legitimized in formal treaties. This, of course, did not save those Indian tribes from mass extermination, torture, or slavery, but it did require that the Europeans clothe these criminal activities with legal procedures so that, from the beginning, the bloody business was legitimized or justified by formal treaties that were acknowledged by all other Western European governments. Similarly, the British veiled their brutal colonization with formal treaties.

Bound by preexisting international treaties, America's founders found it necessary to acknowledge Indian tribes as distinct political entities in the constitutional clause giving Congress the powers "to regulate Commerce with Foreign Nations, and among the several states, and with the Indian Tribes." Thus the Civil Rights Commission report emphasizes that Indian tribes have had a unique, separate legal and political status in American jurisprudence from the very beginning. This clarifies a most damaging and prevalent misconception: that Indian tribes demand fishing rights and other treaty rights solely on the basis of race, in violation of the Fourteenth Amendment to the U.S. Constitution.

The report cites the U.S. Ninth Circuit Court of Appeals, which found that "race was only a factor in determining who was a member of the specific political group that had a treaty agreement with the U.S. Indians who were not members of treaty tribes, had no special rights and, as a race, were subject to fishing laws of the state just like anyone else." As the report goes on to explain, negotiations of treaties with tribes of Washington and Oregon were conducted during peacetime. No wars were fought. The treaties negotiated then were, basically, contracts in which northwest coastal tribes and others gave non-Indians land to settle in exchange for promises of protection from the onslaught of non-Indian settlers and protection of their traditional fishing and hunting practices. Simply stated, the tribes of the northwest kept their part of the bargain and it is high time the federal and state governments kept theirs.

Despite the overwhelming legitimacy and strength of the Indian fishing rights, the commission found that

- The federal government as guarantor of Indian fishing rights has not effectively protected and assured these rights.
- Throughout this century, the state of Washington has

utilized its governmental authority in such a manner as to deprive Indians of their fishing rights.
- Indian tribes have been blamed erroneously for the crisis concerning the scarcity of fish.

The commission findings on land claims, law enforcement, and civil rights for Indian tribes, while they will come as no surprise to Indians, spell out similar violations of Indian rights by federal and state governments. For a carefully documented, step-by-step example of such an outrage, read, on page 95 of the commission's report, how the solicitor general of the United States very nearly lost treaty rights that the Puyallup Indians had spent forty years asserting and defending. This, perhaps, has always been the greatest outrage: that for American Indians, the worst violations came not at the hands of private individuals acting out racist perversions, but from the federal government itself.

Most Americans, while they may not know much about Indian cultures or Indian treaty rights, tend to harbor a special sentiment for American Indians that is not held for other minority groups in America. Whether this is a dim recognition of the fact that Indians were here first or whether it is merely a romantic American notion is difficult to determine. The American public has difficulty believing such injustice continues to be inflicted upon Indian people because Americans assume that the sympathy or tolerance they feel toward Indians is somehow felt or transferred to the government policy that deals with Indians. This is not the case.

For American Indians, injustice has been institutionalized and is administered by federal and state governments. In this regard, the United States is not so different from the racist governments of South Africa and the former Rhodesia. The report observes: "Without wealth or political power, Indian tribes have to rely upon the constitutional-legal system and the moral conscience of society for survival. . . . If this society, through its government, does not live up to its promises and commitments to Indian people, then no rights are secure."

Auntie Kie Talks About U.S. Presidents and U.S. Indian Policy

AUNTIE KIE IS sitting on her old wooden bench in the shade of the tamarisk tree she has named Ida Lupino after her favorite movie star. Auntie Kie is a big woman who holds herself with majesty and ease. Once her children got grown she began spending more time sitting under the tree reading her books on the history of Indian treaties and Indian law. She says she was spending so much time under the tamarisk tree she felt the tree had to have a name. She sits with a flyswatter in one hand and a tall glass of ice and strawberry soda in the other. The flyswatter is mostly for directing the grandchildren who race around her and the backyard on bicycles, pulling the smaller children in a red wagon.

Although she is in her late sixties, Auntie Kie has lost none of her fierce wit. She is always ready to "air her views," as she so delicately puts it. (One of my cousins says what really gets aired are her opponents' views—Auntie Kie shoots them full of holes.) I tell her I have a magazine article to write: what another four years of Ronald Reagan will mean to Native American Indians.

"Oh, *that's* a good one!" Auntie Kie says, laughing so much she nearly spills the soda. But she gets a serious expression on her face, and she says, "That question is different for us Indians than it is for other Americans. It's complicated." I nod my head. That's why I've come to get her answer.

"Well, I don't know. Those people at that magazine might not like what I'm going to tell them." Auntie Kie takes a big swallow of strawberry soda and watches for my reaction. But before I can say anything, Auntie Kie is off and running.

"First, let's get something straight," she says, leaning forward on the bench, jabbing the flyswatter in my direction. "On the day the pilgrims washed up on the East Coast shore, the tribal people of this continent had 1,905,000,000 acres of land. By 1871 the Indians had 140 million acres left. And today, we have 92 million acres, 40 million of which are in Alaska. That's about 5 percent of what we started with, and most of this land is what the white people didn't want.

"So the United States of America, the nation under God indivisible with liberty and justice for all—these United States were founded on stolen land. The descendants of the pilgrims are squatting on Indian land. The so-called Indian treaties were nothing more than frauds, unconscionable contracts that exchanged Indian land for promises white settlers never intended to keep. All of what is called the United States of America, every square inch, is, was, and always will be Indian Country! Because fraud, armed robbery, and murder can't make our land theirs, whatever they try to say!"

Auntie Kie has to fan herself vigorously with the fly-swatter, and she signals one of the grandchildren to bring her more ice and another bottle of strawberry soda. I figure this will be one of my few opportunities to try to steer Auntie Kie back to another four years of Reagan. But as I begin to open my mouth, she sees, and before I can take a breath she is right on me.

"Reagan cuts money for health and education. The whole domestic budget. It hits old people, handicapped people, poor blacks, and poor whites. But for Native Americans these cuts have a whole different dimension. The federal money which used to come to the Indian communities may have been labeled 'assistance.' But for the Native American people, that federal money wasn't 'welfare' or 'aid.' It was money that has been owed to the Indian people for over two hundred years. Another four years of Reagan will only get the United States farther behind in its payments on the Big Debt owed for all the land wrongfully taken and the damages resulting to Native Americans.

"I'll tell the United States of America this: The patience of the sovereign Indian nations is running out. If Reagan gets re-elected, eviction notices will be sent out! They will read: PAY UP OR PACK UP! Oh! You say you can't pay because all your money got loaned out by the greedy bankers to Third World countries who aren't paying it back. Well, we have a modest proposal for you descendants of immigrants and pilgrims: Immigration will be good for you. Head out for Brazil and Argentina and Mexico. Tell them you've been evicted, and you've come to settle on all that real estate the borrowers used for collateral. Those places can probably use all your good Yankee know-how anyway!"

Auntie Kie's expression is fierce, but her eyes are shining, and she pauses to hear my reaction. "But what about the Supreme Court—Reagan could fill four positions," I say valiantly. Auntie Kie doesn't miss a beat. "The United States Constitution says that Congress shall be empowered to regulate all commerce with Indian tribes. That means that the Supreme Court can say whatever it wants, but if the Congress doesn't like it, Congress can change it.

"The best lesson for Native Americans concerning the power of the U.S. Supreme Court came in 1832. The court and the chief justice, John Marshall, held that the state of Georgia could *not* force Cherokee Indians off their lands. The president of the United States, Andrew Jackson, openly defied the court, saying, 'It's the court's decision, let the court enforce it.' Agents of the state of Georgia proceeded to drive the Cherokee people out of the state of Georgia. The Cherokee people lost their businesses and homes. They lost everything. They were marched nearly a thousand miles to alien country over what is now called the Trail of Tears. That's how much the Supreme Court can do for Indians."

"But what if Reagan isn't re-elected—" I say feebly.

"Listen," Auntie Kie cuts in, "you don't lose 1,905,000,000 acres of land only under Republican administrations. I'll tell you something about the American presidency, too. In 1905 Teddy Roosevelt invited Geronimo to ride in his inaugural parade. Quanah Parker from the Comanches was invited. So were leaders from the Utes, Blackfoot, and the Sioux. People who criticized Roosevelt for inviting so-called savage murderers to ride in the inaugural parade were told that the president wished to 'give the people a good show.'"

Auntie Kie flicks away a fly with her swatter. "I think that pretty much says it when it comes to presidents and what good they are to Native Americans or to any other Americans for that matter. American presidents are just there to give the people a good show."

The People and the Land ARE Inseparable

THE PEOPLE AND the land are inseparable, but at first I did not understand. I used to think there were exact boundaries that constituted "the homeland," because I grew up in an age of invisible lines designating ownership. In the old days there had been no boundaries between the people and the land; there had been mutual respect for the land that others were actively using. This respect extended to all living beings, especially to the plants and the animals. We watched our elders behave with respect when they butchered a sheep. The sheep had been raised as a pet and treated with great care and love; when the time came, it was solemn, and the butcher thanked the sheep and reassured it. When the hunter brought home a mule deer buck, the deer occupied the place of honor in the house; it lay on the best Navajo blanket with strings of silver and turquoise beads hanging from its neck; turquoise and silver rings and bracelets decorated the antlers.

What I had not understood was that long ago the people had ranged far and wide all over the desert plateau region. The invisible lines of ownership had divided the land only recently. When I left New Mexico in 1978, I thought I was leaving behind my homeland. My friend Simon J. Ortiz used to telephone me and ask me when I was coming home. But after the first six months, I noticed that the rattlesnakes around the corral and house were quite docile and hospitable, and I realized I *was at home*. By then, too, I had thought much more about the vast Native American diaspora and all the people who had been scattered, taken far from their homelands by the European slave hunters, the survivors who were the last of their kind, who died without ever hearing another word spoken to them in their language.

In Tucson I was not so far from Laguna. One of my best friends and playmates when I was growing up had been Johnie Alonzo, who was half Yaqui. I was in Yaqui country. In the old days there had even been a Laguna man, called Antonio Coyote, who had traveled far to the south for a year or so, but who returned with stories from Mexico City.

I DID NOT really learn about my relationship with the land or know where "home" was until I left Laguna for Tucson. The old folks and the old stories say that the animals and other living beings have a great deal to teach us if we will only pay attention. Because I was unfamiliar with the land around Tucson, I began to pay special attention. The Tucson Mountains are the remains of a huge volcano that exploded long ago; all the rock is shattered and the soil is pale like ash. The fiery clouds of ash and rock melted exotic conglomerates of stone that dazzle the foothills like confetti. I was happy to find such lovely, unusual rocks around my house. I sat on the ground looking at all the wonderful colorful and odd pebbles, and I felt quite at home.

Before I moved to Tucson, I had made one visit, during which my friend Larry Evers took me to an Easter Deer Dance performed at the New Pasqua Yaqui village, located west of Tucson. New Pasqua village was the result of an act of Congress passed in 1973 that recognized the Arizona Yaquis as "American Indians." Until that time, the Yaquis who lived in Arizona were not considered to be Indians, but Mexicans who had fled north to the United States to escape the Mexican Army's genocidal war on Yaquis. Anticipating Hitler's Third Reich by many years, the Mexican Army, under orders, attempted to eradicate the Yaquis. Hundreds of women and children were herded into dry washes or into trenches they were forced to dig at gunpoint, and were shot to death. But long before the appearance of the Europeans, the Yaquis had ranged as far north as Tucson, and it was on this aboriginal use that the United States government based its decision to proclaim Arizona Yaquis American Indians.

After I moved to Tucson, I learned there were two older Yaqui villages within the Tucson metropolitan area, as well as a farming community of Yaquis at Marana, north of Tucson. One Yaqui settlement is located off Twenty-ninth Street and Interstate 10. I don't know its name. The other is located off Grant Road and Interstate 10 and is called Old Pasqua. Although the city of Tucson has sprawled all around these Yaqui settlements, still one can tell immediately where Tucson ends and the Yaqui villages begin. At Old Pasqua, the

Tucson street names suddenly change. Fairview Avenue becomes Calle Central, and the houses become smaller and closer together. The center of the village is a plaza surrounded by a community center, across from a little Catholic church. The little yards are neatly swept, and used building materials, car parts, and firewood are neatly stacked amid fruit trees and little gardens. Corn, beans, melons, roses, zinnias, and sunflowers all grow together; there are no lawns. I was not used to seeing a pueblo within a city. In New Mexico, all but the outlying pueblos were burned, so that Albuquerque, Santa Fe, Los Lunas, and Socorro have no pueblos within their boundaries.

I thought it must be very difficult to exist as a Yaqui village within the city limits of Tucson. These were my thoughts because I had just moved to Tucson from Laguna, and I was thinking about what it means to be separated from one's homeland.

The post office station for my area is located on the edge of Old Pasqua village, so after I had settled in Tucson, I used to find myself driving past Old Pasqua at least once a week. At first I didn't notice anything in particular except the hollyhocks and morning glories or lilacs in bloom. On warm winter days I would see old folks sitting outside with their chairs against the east wall of the house, just as the old folks used to sun themselves at Laguna. After this time, whenever I drove through Old Pasqua I could sense a transition from the city of Tucson to the Yaqui village, where things looked and felt different—more quiet and serene than the apartments and trailer parks just a few blocks away by the post office. In Old Pasqua, no one was in a hurry to go anywhere. People liked to sit or stand outside and talk to their neighbors while the children played leisurely games of catch or rode their bicycles up and down the street. The longer I lived and drove around

Tucson, the more I began to appreciate the sharp contrast between the Yaqui village and the rest of the city. The presence of the Yaqui people and their Yaqui universe with all the spirit beings have consecrated this place; amid all the clamor and pollution of Tucson, this is home.

The Santa Cruz River across Interstate 10 from Old Pasqua flows north out of Mexico past Tucson, to empty into the Gila River, which then flows south. The Santa Cruz flows out of the mountains in Mexico where the Yaqui people still live. Thus the Santa Cruz River makes Old Pasqua home and not exile. I came to realize it was the wishful thinking of Tucson's founding white fathers that had located the Yaquis exclusively in northern Sonora.

One afternoon, after I had been to the post office, I felt like a drive through Old Pasqua. It was about two o'clock, and as I approached the village I didn't see anyone. Even the school grounds at the elementary school were empty. I was thinking to myself how quiet villages are sometimes, how they can seem almost deserted, when suddenly the most amazing scene unfolded before me. At almost the same instant, as if on cue, the doors of nearly all the houses began to open and people of all ages came out. I could hardly believe what I was seeing. I felt a chill, and hair on the back of my neck stood up. A moment before, there had been no one, and now suddenly people of all ages were streaming outside all at once from every house. They were not talking to one another and they did not seem excited or disturbed, but they all were headed in the same direction. When I looked, I saw a white hearse parked in the driveway of one of the houses, and I realized that someone in the village had just passed on. The people were going to comfort their relatives and to pay their respects. What I found amazing then, and what I still marvel at, is the moment all the front doors opened at once. Even if every household had a telephone, and most do not, it would have been quite a feat to orchestrate—to have all the doors open at once and the people step outside.

I understood then that this is what it means to be a people and to be a Yaqui village and not just another Tucson neighborhood. To be a people, to be part of a village, is the dimension of human identity that anthropology understands least, because this sense of home, of the people one comes from, is an intangible quality, not easily understood by American-born Europeans.

The Yaquis may have had to leave behind their Sonoran mountain strongholds, but they did not leave behind their consciousness of their identity as Yaquis, as a people, as a community. This is where their power as a culture lies: with this shared consciousness of being part of a living community that continues on and on, beyond the death of one or even of many, that continues on the riverbanks of the Santa Cruz after the mountains have been left behind.

At Laguna when I was growing up, there were no telephones at all. The town crier still called out at dawn and at dusk the announcements about ditch duty, village meetings, and other communal activities. In the old days the whole village used to participate in communal rabbit hunts. When I was a girl, the town crier would announce the day when everyone was expected to pick up trash and clean up around the village before Laguna Fiesta on September 19 and on the original feast day assigned to San Jose Mission, March 19. A town crier was necessary to remind people about meetings and village work details, but village news and gossip were known and repeated by everyone.

Everyone minded everyone else's business, though they did so quietly, without interference, because to interfere would be bad manners and could cause open confrontations, which the old-time people loathed. At Laguna, when people asked you how you had been lately, they expected to hear all the news and gossip you knew; then they would tell you all the funniest, most shocking, or sad news they had heard. All the gossip and news was told in narratives that often included alleged dialogues with sound effects. The funnier the gossip, the more dramatic the telling. People always remembered other similar incidents, which they would then recount until someone was reminded of a story she had heard, and so on. No matter how funny or sad an incident might be, someone could always recall a similar incident. The effect was to reassure the victim that she was not so isolated by her experience, that others had suffered similar calamities, and that she and her story now were joined with the stories of others just like her. Similarly, a person with great good fortune was not allowed to set himself apart from the rest of the village, because there was always someone who could narrate the details of others who had enjoyed good fortune, again so that the individual did not think himself somehow separate from others just because of his good luck. The storytelling had the effect of placing an incident in the wider context of Pueblo history so that individual loss or failure was less personalized and became part of the village's eternal narratives about loss and failure, narratives that identify the village and that tell the people who they are.

Tribal Councils: Puppets of the U.S. Government

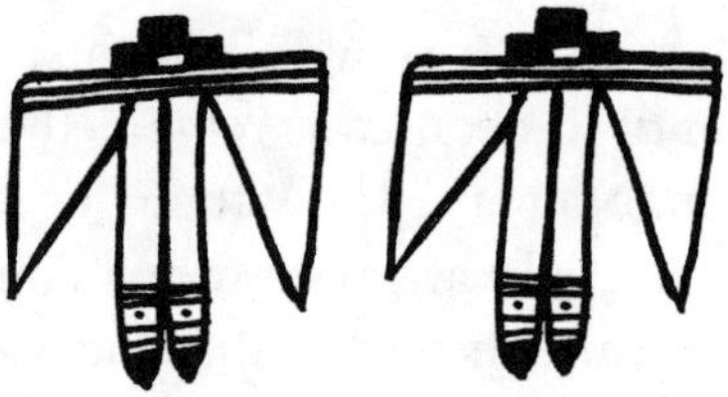

IF THE INDIGENOUS people of the Americas traditionally revered Mother Earth and considered the land and all beings to be sacred, how can it be that the Navajo Tribal Council's own company is deforesting the Chuska Mountains? Aren't the Chuska Mountains sacred mountains? Aren't the Navajos and other Native American communities supposed to revere and protect sacred land? If the Indians care so much about Mother Earth, how come there are strip mines, clear-cut logging, hydroelectric dams, and radioactive waste disposal centers located on Indian land? Is the land no longer sacred to Native Americans?

The answers to these questions lie squarely with the

tribal councils. It is important to understand that the tribal council form of government is not a traditional form of government for the Pueblo or the Navajo people. Instead, the tribal council is an alien form of government that was forced upon the Indian people by the U.S. government in 1941 by the Indian Reorganization Act. The name of the law speaks for itself: the U.S. Congress was not satisfied with the traditional forms of decision making in Indian communities and moved to interfere with Indian tribal governments in 1941 for the convenience of mining and timber interests eager to exploit Indian land. Up until that time, traditional community leaders had opposed such insults to the land and been successful in stopping the mining and timber companies.

Traditionally, among the Navajo and the Pueblo people, decisions were made locally through a consensus of the persons most directly affected by the proposed action. A consensus was reached only after the clan elders had discussed and debated the proposed action with all family and clan members. If a 100 percent consensus could not be reached, then the proposed action was not taken. The people had learned over thousands of years that contentment and harmonious cooperation within the community are far more important to the survival of the people than any short-term gains that aroused dissent or hard feelings.

If the traditional decision-making processes of the Pueblo and Navajo communities had been respected, there would be no strip mines, oil wells, dams, toxic waste disposal, or logging operations on tribal lands. The tribal councils mandated by the 1941 Indian Reorganization Act made it possible to circumvent the traditional decision-making processes of Indian communities and to obtain outcomes deemed favorable by the U.S. Department of the Interior.

Those Indian communities that refused to reorganize

according to the 1941 act were penalized by the U.S. government. Even the most basic nutrition, health, and agricultural aid programs were denied to tribes that did not reorganize. Not surprising, tribal councils usually consist of so-called progressives, or acculturated individuals of the Indian communities, persons who had been brainwashed in Bureau of Indian Affairs schools or missionary schools. Like its white father, the U.S. Congress, the tribal council form of government offers easy access to influence peddlers but fails to protect the local people most affected by its decisions.

The constitutionality of coercing Indian tribes to abandon their traditional governments for puppet governments called tribal councils has not been tested in court, but someday the issue will arise, and hundreds of thousands of grazing leases, mining and timber leases on Indian land will be invalidated. International law and the U.S. Constitution bar the U.S. government from interfering with the sovereign tribal governments of the Native Americans. The day will come when the political tides will turn and hundreds of years of infamy will be redressed.

All places and all beings of the earth are sacred. It is dangerous to designate some places sacred when all are sacred. Such compromises imply that there is a hierarchy of value, with some places and some living beings not as important as others. No part of the earth is expendable; the earth is a whole that cannot be fragmented, as it has been by the destroyers' mentality of the industrial age. The greedy destroyers of life and bringers of suffering demand that sacred land be sacrificed so that a few designated sacred places may survive; but once any part is deemed expendable, others can easily be redefined to fit the category of expendable. As Ruth Rudner points out in her article "Sacred Land," what spiritual replenishment is possible if one must travel through ghastly fumes and ravaged lands to reach the little island or ocean or mountain that has been preserved by the label *sacred land?*

There can be no compromises with these serial killers of life on earth because they are so sick they can't stop themselves. They would like the rest of us to embrace death as they have, to say, "Well, all this is dead already, what will it matter if they are permitted to kill a little more?" Even among the conservation groups there is an unfortunate value system in place that writes off or sacrifices some locations because they are no longer "virgin." Those who claim to love and protect the Mother Earth have to love all of her, even the places that are no longer pristine. Ma ah shra true ee, the giant serpent messenger, chose the edge of the uranium mining tailings at Jackpile Mine for his reappearance; he was making this point when he chose that unlikely location. The land has not been desecrated; human beings desecrate only themselves.

The Mother Earth is inviolable.

Hunger Stalked the Tribal People

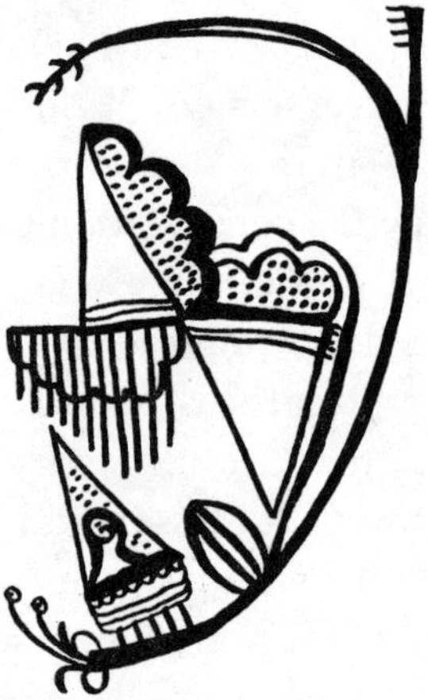

HUNGER STALKED THE tribal people of the southwest even into the twentieth century when the U.S. government imprisoned the people for refusing to send their small children away to boarding schools. With a critical part of their workforce in jail, the remaining people could not give the corn and bean plants all the care that was necessary; the crops failed and the people starved. U.S. government policies still cause people to go hungry on and off Indian reservations.

A child who wasted food was sternly admonished, and the old stories were told about drought years and starvation. Before anyone at the dinner table would take a bite, everyone would silently give thanks to all of the animal and plant beings that had given themselves to human beings to stop the hunger. A small pottery bowl was passed around the table at the same time, and the smallest child was encouraged to take small pinches from the food on her plate to feed to the spirits of beloved family members. No meal is ever eaten without first saying thanks. No person, no stranger who arrived at mealtime was ever refused, even if everyone else had a bit less on the plate, because the sharing of food is a fundamental expression of humanity. Hungry animals eat first and allow others to feed only when they have filled themselves; even mother coyotes or mother hawks swallow the food first and regurgitate later. To share one's food is to demonstrate one's humanity. So each meal at Laguna was an occasion for thanksgiving, and each meal was shared with everyone, even strangers.

Long ago, when the Navajo and Apache people first migrated south, they had a difficult time adapting to the weather and the terrain. The Pueblo people did what they could to help the newcomers learn the ways of the land, but some years the Navajos had meager harvests, and then they would face starvation. At first, the starving people would make raids to steal food from the Pueblo storehouses. No one would be killed or injured in the raids, but the Pueblo villages would be terribly upset, and the people would have to send out parties of warriors to try to recover the lost food or livestock.

My great-grandmother was so proud of the way the people solved this crisis. Her grandfather and the other men from Laguna managed to catch up with the Navajo raiders because the raiders were trying to flee with a herd of sheep. The raiders were some older men and a couple of boys, and when the party from Laguna stopped them, the raiders expected to get roughed up. The Lagunas asked the raiders why they had stolen the sheep, and the raiders said that back at their home the people were starving to death, and they didn't know what else to do. The Laguna party separated four sheep from the herd and told the raiders to take them, and next time, when the people were hungry, just to come and ask for food, and the Lagunas would give them some.

Thus during the summer months and at harvest time, the Pueblo people still celebrate feast days when thanks are given to the spirits for the food, and Navajos, Apaches, and other people outside the pueblos are welcome. During the feast days, strangers must be invited to sit down and eat at any house the stranger may come to. Over the years, friendships developed between certain individuals, and gifts were exchanged. One of the saddest times during the months after my Grandpa Hank died came at Laguna feast time when the old Navajo man from Alamo who was Grandpa's friend asked for Grandpa. The old man wept when he learned Grandpa was dead.

Once a year, the U.S. celebrates Thanksgiving and traces the day back to the year the starving pilgrims were fed by the Indians, who no doubt realized that hungry pilgrims, like all hungry human beings, might be dangerous. It isn't great spirituality or generosity but simple human intelligence that says that when some are well fed and some are hungry, the hungry people must be fed; otherwise there can be no peace or security for those with the food.

It is interesting that the old pagan European celebration of All Hallows' Eve is celebrated in the U.S. only a few weeks before Thanksgiving. Ancient Europeans had to feed the spirits of their dead ancestors and the living who were hungry enough to masquerade as dead souls; and if they didn't feed them, they expected reprisals—thus the saying "Trick or treat." Every day in the U.S. should be Thanksgiving Day, with baskets of food and turkey dinners for the hungry; otherwise, every night in the U.S. might be "Trick or Treat," and it won't just be hungry ghosts of ancestors playing the tricks.

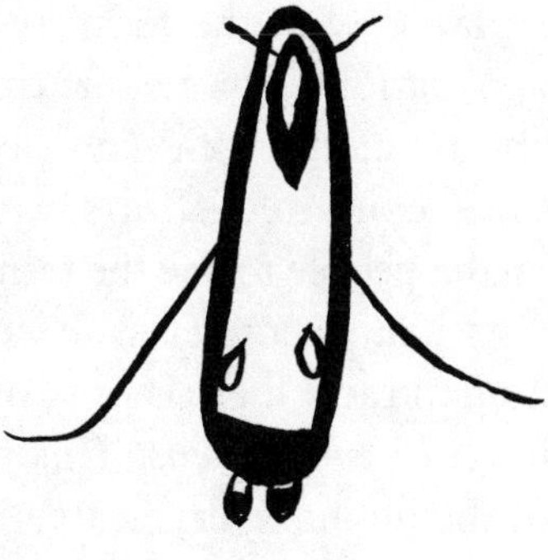

Fences Against Freedom

As a person of mixed ancestry, I have always been very sensitive to the prevailing attitudes toward people of color. I remember a time around 1965 when the term *race* was nearly replaced with the term *ancestry* on government forms and applications. For a short time questions about one's ancestry and religion were even deleted from paperwork. During this time, concerted efforts were made by public officials and media people to use the term *ancestry* instead of *race*. Geneticists had scientific evidence that there is only one race, the human race; there is only one species to which all people belong: *Homo sapiens*. This period of conscientious education of the public to eradicate misinformation about "race" grew out of the civil rights movement of the 1950s and from key decisions from the U.S. Supreme Court. Presidents Kennedy and Johnson spoke explicitly about the blot on the honor of the U.S. made by centuries of prejudice; even the U.S. Congress, with the exception of a few senators and congressmen from southern states, joined them in asserting equality for all human beings.

In 1967 I chose "race" as my topic for a paper in one of my college honors seminars. I had taken two semesters of anthropology in my freshman year, and I already knew that "race" had been a hot topic among the physical anthropologists for decades. I understood that the "one race, human race" theorists like Ashley Montagu had finally assembled incontrovertible biological proofs that had swept away the nineteenth-century theories of distinct "races." But I wanted to see exactly how this shift had come about, because I knew that many people still were under the influence of nineteenth-century notions concerning race.

I went to the University of New Mexico library and checked out all the books I could find on the topic of "race." As a person of mixed ancestry, I could not afford to take my anthropology professor or Ashley Montagu's word for it. Segregationists implied that liberals had seized power on campuses and that to mollify blacks and other "racial" minorities these liberals had concocted false data to prove human equality. My parents and the people of the Laguna Pueblo community who raised me taught me that we are all one family—all the offspring of Mother Earth—and no one is better or worse according to skin color or origin. My whole life I had believed this, but now I had to test what I had been taught as a child because I had also been taught that the truth matters more than anything, even more than personal comfort, more than one's own vanity. It was possible that my parents and the people at home, along with people like Ashley Montagu, had deluded themselves just as the segregationists had alleged. I was determined to know the truth even if the truth was unpleasant.

I don't remember all the books I read, but I do remember that Carleton Coon was the name of the leading physical anthropologist whose books and articles argued the "racial superiority" of some "races" over others. I wondered then if Mr. Coon's vehemence about the superiority of the white race had anything to do with his name, which I knew was a common slur used against African Americans. Had the other children teased him about his name in the school yard? Was that why Coon had endured censure by his peers to persist in his "race" research in physical anthropology long after the Nuremberg trials?

I once read an article whose author stated that racism is the only form of mental illness that is communicable. Clever but not entirely true. Racism in the U.S. is learned by us beginning at birth.

As a person of mixed ancestry growing up in the United States in the late 1950s, I knew all of the cruel epithets that might be hurled at others; the knowledge was a sort of solace that I was not alone in my feelings of unease, of not quite belonging to the group that clearly mattered most in the United States.

Human beings need to feel as if they "belong"; I learned from my father to feel comfortable and happy alone in the mesas and hills around Laguna. It was not so easy for me to learn where we Marmons belonged, but gradually I understood that we of mixed ancestry belonged on the outer edge of the circle between the world of the Pueblo and the outside world. The Laguna people were open and accepted children of mixed ancestry because appearance was secondary to behavior. For the generation of my great-grandmother and earlier generations, anyone who had not been born in the community was a stranger, regardless of skin color. Strangers were not judged by their appearances—which could deceive—but by their behavior. The old-time people took their time to become acquainted with a person before they made a judgment. The old-time people were very secure in themselves and their identity; and thus they were able to appreciate differences and to even marvel at personal idiosyncrasies so long as no one and nothing was being harmed.

The cosmology of the Pueblo people is all-inclusive; long before the arrival of the Spaniards in the Americas, the Pueblo and other indigenous communities knew that the Mother Creator had many children in faraway places. The ancient stories include all people of the earth, so when the Spaniards marched into Laguna in 1540, the inclination still was to include rather than to exclude the strangers, even though the people had heard frightening stories and rumors about the white men. My great-grandmother and the people of her generation were always very curious and took delight in learning odd facts and strange but true stories. The old-time people believed that we must keep learning as much as we can all of our lives. So the people set out to learn if there was anything at all *good* in these strangers; because they had never met any humans who were completely evil. Sure enough, it was true with these strangers too; some of them had evil hearts, but many were good human beings.

Similarly, when my great-grandfather, a white man, married into the Anaya family, he was adopted into the community by his wife's family and clans. There always had been political factions among these families and clans, and by his marriage, my great-grandfather became a part of the political intrigues at Laguna. Some accounts by anthropologists attempt to portray my great-grandfather and his brother as instigators or meddlers, but the anthropologists have overestimated their importance and their tenuous position in the Pueblo. Naturally, the factions into which the Marmon brothers had married incorporated these new "sons" into their ongoing intrigues and machinations. But the anthropologists who would portray the Marmon brothers as dictators fool themselves about the power of white men in a pueblo. The minute the Marmon brothers crossed over the line, they would have been killed.

Indeed, people at Laguna remember my great-grandfather as a gentle, quiet man, while my beloved Grandma A'mooh is remembered as a stern, formidable woman who ran the show. She was also a Presbyterian. Her family, the Anayas, had kept cattle and sheep for a long time, and I imagine that way back in the past, an ancestor of hers had been curious about the odd animals the strangers brought and decided to give them a try.

I was fortunate to be reared by my great-grandmother and others of her generation. They always took an interest in us children and they were always delighted to answer our questions and to tell us stories about the old days. Although there were very few children of mixed ancestry in those days, the old folks did not seem to notice. But I could sense a difference from younger people, the generation that had gone to the First World War. On rare occasions, I could sense an anger that my appearance stirred in them, although I sensed that the anger was not aimed at me personally. My appearance reminded them of the outside world, where racism was thriving.

I learned about racism firsthand from the Marmon family. My great-grandfather endured the epithet Squaw Man. Once when he and two of his young sons (my Grandpa Hank and his brother Frank) walked through the lobby of Albuquerque's only hotel to reach the café inside, the hotel manager stopped my great-grandfather. He told my great-grandfather that he was welcome to walk through the lobby, but when he had Indians with him, he should use the back door. My great-grandfather informed him that the "Indians" were his sons, and then he left and never went into the hotel again.

There were branches of the Marmon family that, although Laguna, still felt they were better than the rest of us Marmons and the rest of the Lagunas as well. Grandpa Hank's sister, Aunt Esther, was beautiful and vain and light skinned; she boarded at the Sherman Institute in Riverside, California, where my grandfather and other Indian students were taught trades. But Aunt Esther did not get along with the other Indian girls; she refused to speak to them or to have anything to do with them. So she was allowed to attend a Riverside girls school with white girls. My grandfather, who had a broad nose and face and "looked Indian," told the counselor at Sherman that he wanted to become an automobile designer. He was told by the school guidance counselor that Indians weren't able to design automobiles; they taught him to be a store clerk.

I learned about racism firsthand when I started school. We were punished if we spoke the Laguna language once we crossed onto the school grounds. Every fall, all of us were lined up and herded like cattle to the girls' and boys' bathrooms, where our heads were drenched with smelly insecticide regardless of whether we had lice or not. We were vaccinated in both arms without regard to our individual immunization records.

But what I remember most clearly is the white tourists who used to come to the school yard to take our pictures.

They would give us kids each a nickel, so naturally when we saw tourists get out of their cars with cameras, we all wanted to get in the picture. Then one day when I was older, in the third grade, white tourists came with cameras. All of my playmates started to bunch together to fit in the picture, and I was right there with them maneuvering myself into the group when I saw the tourist look at me with a particular expression. I knew instantly he did not want me to be in the picture; I stayed close to my playmates, hoping that I had misread the man's face. But the tourist motioned for me to move away to one side, out of his picture. I remember my playmates looked puzzled, but I knew why the man did not want me in his picture: I looked different from my playmates. I was part white and he didn't want me to spoil his snapshots of "Indians." After that incident, the arrival of tourists with cameras at our school filled me with anxiety. I would stand back and watch the expressions on the tourists' faces before trying to join my playmates in the picture. Most times the tourists were kindly and did not seem to notice my difference, and they would motion for me to join my classmates; but now and then there were tourists who looked relieved that I did not try to join in the group picture.

Racism is a constant factor in the United States; it is always in the picture even if it only forms the background. Now as the condition of the U.S. economy continues to deteriorate and the people grow restive with the U.S. Congress and the president, the tactics of party politicians sink deeper in corruption. Racism is now a trump card, to be played again and again shamelessly by both major political parties. The U.S. government applications that had used the term *ancestry* disappeared; the fiction of "the races" has been reestablished. Soon after Nixon's election the changes began, and racism became a key component once more in the U.S.

political arena. The Republican Party found the issue of race to be extremely powerful, so the Democrats, desperate for power, have also begun to pander racism to the U.S. electorate.

Fortunately, the people of the United States are far better human beings than the greedy elected officials who allegedly represent them in Congress and the White House. The elected officials of both parties currently are trying to whip up hysteria over immigration policy in the most blatantly racist manner. Politicians and media people talk about the "illegal aliens" to dehumanize and demonize undocumented immigrants, who are for the most part people of color. The Cold War with the Communist world is over, and now the military defense contractors need to create a new bogeyman to justify U.S. defense spending. The U.S.-Mexico border is fast becoming a militarized zone. The army and marine units from all over the U.S. come to southern Arizona to participate in "training exercises" along the border.

When I was growing up, U.S. politicians called Russia an "Iron Curtain" country, which implied terrible shame. As I got older I learned that there wasn't really a curtain made of iron around the Soviet Union; I was later disappointed to learn that the wall in Berlin was made of concrete, not iron. Now the U.S. government is building a steel wall twelve feet high that eventually will span the entire length of the Mexican border. The steel wall already spans four-mile sections of the border at Mexicali and Naco; and at Nogales, sixty miles south of Tucson, the steel wall is under construction.

Immigration and Naturalization Services, or the Border Patrol, has greatly expanded its manpower and checkpoint stations. Now when you drive down Interstate 10 toward El Paso, you will find a check station. When you drive north from Las Cruces up I-25 about ten miles north of Truth or

Consequences, all interstate highway traffic is diverted off the highway into an INS checkpoint. I was detained at that checkpoint in December 1991 on my way from Tucson to Albuquerque for a book signing of my novel *Almanac of the Dead.* My companion and I were detained despite the fact that we showed the Border Patrol our Arizona driver's licenses. Two men from California, both Chicanos, were being detained at the same time, despite the fact that they too presented an ID and spoke English without the thick Texas accents of the Border Patrolmen. While we were detained, we watched as other vehicles were waved through the checkpoint. The occupants of those vehicles were white. It was quite clear that my appearance—my skin color—was the reason for the detention.

The Border Patrol exercises a power that no highway patrol or county sheriff possesses: the Border Patrol can detain anyone they wish for no reason at all. A policeman or sheriff needs to have some shred of probable cause, but not the Border Patrol. In fact, they stop people with Indio-Hispanic characteristics, and they target cars in which white people travel with brown people. Recent reports of illegal immigration by people of Asian ancestry mean that the Border Patrol now routinely detain anyone who looks Asian. Once you have been stopped at a Border Patrol checkpoint, you are under the control of the Border Patrol agent; the refusal to obey any order by the Border Patrol agent means you have broken the law and may be arrested for failure to obey a federal officer. Once the car is stopped, they ask you to step out of the car; then they ask you to open the trunk. If you ask them why or request a search warrant, they inform you that it will take them three or four hours to obtain a search warrant. They make it very clear that if you "force" them to get a search warrant, they will strip-search your body as well as your car and luggage. On this particular day I was due in Albuquerque, and I did not have the four hours to spare. So I opened my car trunk, but not without using my right to free speech to tell them what I thought of them and their police state procedures. "You are not wanted here," I shouted at them, and they seemed astonished. "Only a few years ago we used to be able to move freely within our own country," I said. "This is our home. Take all this back where you came from. You are not wanted here."

Scarcely a year later, my friend and I were driving south from Albuquerque, returning to Tucson after a paperback book promotion. There are no Border Patrol detention areas on the southbound lanes of I-25, so I settled back and went to sleep while Gus drove. I awakened when I felt the car slowing to a stop. It was nearly midnight on New Mexico State Road 26, a dark lonely stretch of two-lane highway between Hatch and Deming. When I sat up, I saw the headlights and emergency flashers of six vehicles—Border Patrol cars and a Border Patrol van blocked both lanes of the road. Gus stopped the car and rolled down his window to ask what was wrong. But the Border Patrolman and his companion did not reply; instead the first officer ordered us to "step out of the car." Gus asked why we had to get out of the car. His question seemed to set them off—two more Border Patrolmen immediately approached the car and one of them asked, "Are you looking for trouble?" as if he would relish the opportunity.

I will never forget that night beside the highway. There was an awful feeling of menace and of violence straining to break loose. It was clear that they would be happy to drag us out of the car if we did not comply. So we both got out of the car and they motioned for us to stand on the shoulder of the road. The night was very dark, and no other traffic had come down the road since they had stopped us. I thought how easy it would be for the Border Patrolmen to shoot us and leave our bodies and car beside the road. There were two other Border Patrolmen by the van. The man who had asked if we were looking for trouble told his partner to "get the dog," and from the back of the white van another Border Patrolman brought a small female German shepherd on a leash. The dog did not heel well enough to suit him, and I saw the dog's handler jerk the leash. They opened the doors of our car and pulled the dog's head into the car, but I saw immediately from the expression in her eyes that the dog hated them, and she would not serve them. When she showed no interest in the inside of the car, they brought her around back to the trunk, near where we were standing. They half-dragged her up into the trunk, but still she did not indicate stowed-away humans or illegal drugs.

Their mood got uglier; they seemed outraged that the dog could not find any contraband, and they dragged her over to us and commanded her to sniff our legs and feet. To my relief, the strange anger the INS agents had focused at us now had shifted to the dog. I no longer felt so strongly that we would be murdered. We exchanged looks—the dog and I. She was afraid of what they might do, just as I was. The handler jerked the leash violently as she sniffed us, as if to make her perform better, but the dog refused to accuse us. The dog had an innate dignity, an integrity that did not permit her to serve those men. I can't forget the expression in her eyes; it was as if she was embarrassed to be associated with them. I had a small amount of medicinal marijuana in my purse that night, but the dog refused to expose me. I am not partial to dogs, but I can't forget the small German shepherd. She saved us from the strange murderous mood of the Border Patrolmen that night.

In February of 1993, I was invited by the Women's Studies Department at UCLA to be a distinguished visiting lecturer. After I had described my run-ins with the Border Patrol, a professor of history at UCLA related her story. It seems she had been traveling by train from Los Angeles to Albuquerque twice each month to work with an informant. She had noticed that the Border Patrol officers were there each week to meet the Amtrak trains to scrutinize the passengers, but since she is six feet tall and of Irish and German ancestry, she was not particularly concerned. Then one day when she stepped off the train in Albuquerque, two Border Patrolmen accosted her. They wanted to know what she was doing, why she was traveling between Los Angeles and Albuquerque. This is the sort of police state that has developed in the southwest United States. No person, no citizen is free to travel without the scrutiny of the Border Patrol. Because Reverend Fife and the sanctuary movement bring political refugees into the U.S. from Central America, the Border Patrol is suspicious of and detains white people who appear to be clergy, those who wear ethnic clothing or jewelry, and women who wear very long hair or very short hair (they could be nuns). Men with beards and men with long hair are also likely to be detained because INS agents suspect "those sorts" of white people may help political refugees.

In Phoenix the INS agents raid public high schools and drag dark-skinned students away to their vans. In 1992, in El Paso, Texas, a high school football coach driving a vanload of his players in full uniform was pulled over on the freeway and INS agents put a cocked revolver to the coach's head through the van window. That incident was one of many similar abuses by the INS in the El Paso area that finally resulted in a restraining order against the Border Patrol issued by a federal judge in El Paso.

At about the same time, a Border Patrol agent in Nogales shot an unarmed undocumented immigrant in the back one night and attempted to hide the body; a few weeks earlier the same Border Patrol agent had shot and wounded another undocumented immigrant. His fellow agent, perhaps realizing Agent Elmer had gone around the bend, refused to help in the cover-up, so Agent Elmer threatened him. Agent Elmer was arrested and tried for murder, but his southern Arizona jury empathized with his fear of brown-skinned people; they believed Agent Elmer's story that he feared for his life even though the victim was shot in the back trying to flee. Agent Elmer was also cleared of the charges of wounding in the other case. For years, undocumented immigrant women have reported sexual assaults by Border Patrol agents. But it wasn't until Agent Elmer was tried for murder that another Nogales INS agent was convicted of the rape of a woman he had taken into custody for detainment. In the city of South Tucson, where 80 percent of the respondents were Chicano or Mexicano, a research project by the University of Wisconsin recently revealed that one out of every five persons living there had been stopped by INS agents in the past year.

I no longer feel the same about driving from Tucson to Albuquerque via the southern route. For miles before I approach the INS check stations, I can feel the anxiety pressing hard against my chest. But I feel anger too, a deep, abiding anger at the U.S. government, and I know that I am not alone in my hatred of these racist immigration policies, which are broadcast every day, teaching racism, demonizing all people of color, labeling indigenous people from Mexico as "aliens"—creatures not quite human.

The so-called civil wars in El Salvador and Guatemala are actually wars against the indigenous tribal people conducted by the white and mestizo ruling classes. These are genocidal wars conducted to secure Indian land once and for all. The Mexican government is buying Black Hawk helicopters in preparation for the eradication of the Zapatistas after the August elections.

I blame the U.S. government—congressmen and senators and President Clinton. I blame Clinton most of all for playing the covert racism card marked "Immigration Policy." The elected officials, blinded by greed and ambition, show great disrespect to the electorate they represent. The people, the ordinary people in the street, evidence only a fraction of the racist behavior that is exhibited on a daily basis by the elected leaders of the United States and their sluttish handmaidens, the big television networks.

If we truly had a representative democracy in the United States, I do not think we would see such a shameful level of racism in this country. But so long as huge amounts of money are necessary in order to run for office, we will not have a representative democracy. The form of government we have in the United States right now is not representative democracy but "big capitalism"; big capitalism can't survive for long in the United States unless the people are divided among themselves into warring factions. Big capitalism wants the people of the United States to blame "foreigners" for lost jobs and declining living standards so the people won't place the blame where it really belongs: with our corrupt U.S. Congress and president.

As I prepare to drive to New Mexico this week, I feel a prickle of anxiety down my spine. Only a few years ago, I used to travel the highways between Arizona and New Mexico with a wonderful sensation of absolute freedom as I cruised down the open road and across the vast desert plateaus in southern Arizona and southern New Mexico. We citizens of the United States grew up believing this freedom of the open road to be our inalienable right. The freedom of the open road meant we could travel freely from state to state without special papers or threat of detainment; this was a "right" citizens of Communist and totalitarian governments did not possess. That wide open highway was what told us we were U.S. citizens. Indeed, some say, this freedom to travel is an integral part of the American identity.

To deny this right to me, to some of us who because of skin color or other physical characteristics appear to fit fictional profiles of "undesirables," is to begin the inexorable slide into further government-mandated "race policies" that can only end in madness and genocide. The slaughters in Rwanda and Bosnia did not occur spontaneously—with neighbor butchering neighbor out of the blue; no, politicians and government officials called down these maelstroms of blood on their people by unleashing the terrible irrational force that racism is.

Take a drive down Interstate 8 or Interstate 10, along the U.S.-Mexico border. Notice the Border Patrol checkpoints all vehicles must pass through. When the Border Patrol agent asks you where you are coming from and where you are going, don't kid around and answer in Spanish—you could be there all afternoon. Look south into Mexico and enjoy the view while you are still able, before you find yourself behind the twelve-foot steel curtain the U.S. government is building.

My late-night, dark road encounter with the Border Patrol was so disturbing that I wrote about it again, in an essay that focuses exclusively on immigration policy and recent incidents in the Tucson area.

The Border Patrol State

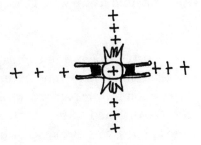

I USED TO travel the highways of New Mexico and Arizona with a wonderful sensation of absolute freedom as I cruised down the open road and across the vast desert plateaus. On the Laguna Pueblo reservation, where I was raised, the people were patriotic despite the way the U.S. government had treated Native Americans. As proud citizens, we grew up believing the freedom to travel was our inalienable right, a right that some Native Americans had been denied in the early twentieth century. Our cousin old Bill Pratt used to ride his horse three hundred miles overland from Laguna, New Mexico, to Prescott, Arizona, every summer to work as a fire lookout.

In school in the 1950s, we were taught that our right to travel from state to state without special papers or threat of detainment was a right that citizens under Communist and totalitarian governments did not possess. That wide open highway told us we were U.S. citizens; we were free . . .

NOT SO LONG ago, my companion Gus and I were driving south from Albuquerque, returning to Tucson after a book promotion for the paperback edition of my novel *Almanac of the Dead.* I had settled back and gone to sleep while Gus drove, but I was awakened when I felt the car slowing to a stop. It was nearly midnight on New Mexico State Road 26, a dark, lonely stretch of two-lane highway between Hatch and Deming. When I sat up, I saw the headlights and emergency flashers of six vehicles—Border Patrol cars and a van were blocking both lanes of the highway. Gus stopped the car and rolled down the window to ask what was wrong. But the closest Border Patrolman and his companion did not reply; instead, the first agent ordered us to "step out of the car." Gus asked why, but his question seemed to set them off. Two more Border Patrol agents immediately approached our car, and one of them snapped, "Are you looking for trouble?" as if he would relish it.

I will never forget that night beside the highway. There was an awful feeling of menace and violence straining to break loose. It was clear that the uniformed men would be only too happy to drag us out of the car if we did not speedily comply with their request (asking a question is tantamount to resistance, it seems). So we stepped out of the car and they motioned for us to stand on the shoulder of the road. The night was very dark, and no other traffic had come down the road since we had been stopped. All I could think about was a book I had read—*Nunca Más*—the official report of a human rights commission that investigated and certified more than twelve thousand "disappearances" during Argentina's "dirty war" in the late 1970s.

The weird anger of these Border Patrolmen made me think about descriptions in the report of Argentine police and military officers who became addicted to interrogation, torture, and the murder that followed. When the military and police ran out of political suspects to torture and kill, they resorted to the random abduction of citizens off the streets. I thought how easy it would be for the Border Patrol to shoot us and leave our bodies and car beside the highway, like so many bodies found in these parts and ascribed to drug runners.

Two other Border Patrolmen stood by the white van. The one who had asked if we were looking for trouble ordered his partner to "get the dog," and from the back of the van another patrolman brought a small female German shepherd on a leash. The dog apparently did not heel well enough to suit him, and the handler jerked the leash. They opened the doors of our car and pulled the dog's head into it, but I saw immediately from the expression in her eyes that the dog hated them and that she would not serve them. When she showed no interest in the inside of our car, they brought her around back to the trunk, near where we were standing. They half-dragged her up into the trunk, but still she did not indicate any stowed-away human beings or illegal drugs.

Their mood got uglier; the officers seemed outraged that the dog could not find any contraband, and they dragged her over to us and commanded her to sniff our legs and feet. To my relief, the strange violence the Border Patrol agents had focused on us now seemed shifted to the dog. I no longer felt so strongly that we would be murdered. We exchanged looks—the dog and I. She was afraid of what they might do, just as I was. The dog's handler jerked the leash sharply as she sniffed us, as if to make her perform better, but the dog refused to accuse us; she had an innate dignity that did not permit her to serve the murderous impulses of those men. I can't forget the expression in the dog's eyes; it was as if she were embarrassed to be associated with them. I had a small amount of medicinal marijuana in my purse that night, but she refused to expose me. I am not partial to dogs, but I will always remember the small German shepherd that night.

Unfortunately, what happened to me is an everyday occurrence here now. Since the 1980s, on top of greatly expanding border checkpoints, the Immigration and Naturalization Service and the Border Patrol have implemented policies that interfere with the rights of U.S. citizens to travel freely within our borders. INS agents now patrol all interstate highways and roads that lead to or from the U.S.-Mexico border in Texas, New Mexico, Arizona, and California. Now, when you drive east from Tucson on Interstate 10 toward El Paso, you encounter an INS check station outside Las Cruces, New Mexico. When you drive north from Las Cruces up Interstate 25, two miles north of the town of Truth or Consequences, the highway is blocked with orange emergency barriers, and all traffic is diverted into a two-lane Border Patrol checkpoint—ninety-five miles north of the U.S.-Mexico border.

I was detained once at Truth or Consequences, despite my and my companion's Arizona driver's licenses. Two men, both Chicanos, were detained at the same time, despite the fact that they too presented ID and spoke English without the thick Texas accents of the Border Patrol agents. While we were stopped, we watched as other vehicles—whose occupants were white—were waved through the checkpoint.

White people traveling with brown people, however, can expect to be stopped on suspicion they work with the sanctuary movement, which shelters refugees. White people who appear to be clergy, those who wear ethnic clothing or jewelry, and women with very long hair or very short hair (they could be nuns) are also frequently detained; white men with beards or men with long hair are likely to be detained, too, because Border Patrol agents have profiles of "those sorts" of white people who may help political refugees. (Most of the political refugees from Guatemala and El Salvador are Native American or mestizo because the indigenous people of the Americas have continued to resist efforts by invaders to displace them from their ancestral lands.) Alleged increases in illegal immigration by people of Asian ancestry mean that the Border Patrol now routinely detains anyone who appears to be Asian or part Asian, as well.

Once your car is diverted from the interstate highway into the checkpoint area, you are under the control of the Border Patrol, which in practical terms exercises a power that no highway patrol or city patrolman possesses: they are willing to detain anyone, for no apparent reason. Other law-enforcement officers need a shred of probable cause in order to detain someone. On the books, so does the Border Patrol; but on the road, it's another matter. They'll order you to stop your car and step out; then they'll ask you to open the trunk. If you ask why or request a search warrant, you'll be told that they'll have to have a dog sniff the car before they can request a search warrant, and the dog might not get there for two or three hours. The search warrant might require an hour or two past that. They make it clear that if you force them to obtain a search warrant for the car, they will make you submit to a strip search as well.

Traveling in the open, though, the sense of violation can

be even worse. Never mind high-profile cases like that of former Border Patrol agent Michael Elmer, acquitted of murder by claiming self-defense, despite admitting that as an officer he shot an illegal immigrant in the back and then hid the body, which remained undiscovered until another Border Patrolman reported the event. (Last month, Elmer was convicted of reckless endangerment in a separate incident, for shooting at least ten rounds from his M-16 too close to a group of immigrants as they were crossing illegally into Nogales in March 1992.) Never mind that in El Paso, a high school football coach driving a vanload of his players in full uniform was pulled over on the freeway and a Border Patrol agent put a cocked revolver to his head. (The football coach was Mexican-American, as were most of the players in his van; the incident eventually caused a federal judge to issue a restraining order against the Border Patrol.) We've a mountain of personal experiences like that that never make the newspapers. A history professor at UCLA told me she had been traveling by train from Los Angeles to Albuquerque twice a month doing research. On each of her trips, she had noticed that the Border Patrol agents were at the station in Albuquerque scrutinizing the passengers. Since she is six feet tall and of Irish and German ancestry, she was not particularly concerned. Then one day when she stepped off the train in Albuquerque, two Border Patrolmen accosted her, wanting to know what she was doing, and why she was traveling between Los Angeles and Albuquerque twice a month. She presented identification and an explanation deemed suitable by the agents and was allowed to go about her business.

Just the other day, I mentioned to a friend that I was writing this article and he told me about his seventy-three-year-old father, who is half Chinese and had set out alone by car from Tucson to Albuquerque the week before. His father had become confused by road construction and missed a turnoff from Interstate 10 to Interstate 25; when he turned around and circled back, he missed the turnoff a second time. But when he looped back for yet another try, Border Patrol agents stopped him and forced him to open his trunk. After they satisfied themselves that he was not smuggling Chinese immigrants, they sent him on his way. He was so rattled by the event that he had to be driven home by his daughter.

This is the police state that has developed in the southwestern United States since the 1980s. No person, no citizen, is free to travel without the scrutiny of the Border Patrol. In the city of South Tucson, where 80 percent of the respondents were Chicano or Mexicano, a joint research project by the University of Wisconsin and the University of Arizona recently concluded that one out of every five people there had been detained, mistreated verbally or nonverbally, or questioned by INS agents in the past two years.

MANIFEST DESTINY MAY lack its old grandeur of theft and blood—"lock the door" is what it means now, with racism a trump card to be played again and again, shamelessly, by both major political parties. "Immigration," like "street crime" and "welfare fraud," is a political euphemism that refers to people of color. Politicians and media people talk about "illegal aliens" to dehumanize and demonize undocumented immigrants, who are for the most part people of color. Even in the days of Spanish and Mexican rule, no attempts were made to interfere with the flow of people and goods from south to north and north to south. It is the U.S. government that has continually attempted to sever contact between the tribal people north of the border and those to the south.[1]

Now that the "Iron Curtain" is gone, it is ironic that the U.S. government and its Border Patrol are constructing a steel wall ten feet high to span sections of the border with Mexico. While politicians and multinational corporations extol the virtues of NAFTA and free trade (in goods, not flesh), the ominous curtain is already up in a six-mile section at the border crossing at Mexicali; two miles are being erected but are not yet finished at Naco; and at Nogales, sixty miles south of Tucson, the steel wall has been all rubber-stamped and awaits construction, likely to begin in March. Like the pathetic multimillion-dollar antidrug border surveillance balloons that were continually deflated by high winds and made only a couple of meager interceptions before they blew away, the fence along the border is a theatrical prop, a bit of pork for contractors. Border entrepreneurs have already used blowtorches to cut passageways through the fence to collect "tolls" and are doing a brisk business. Back in Washington, the INS announces a $300 million computer contract to modernize its record keeping and Congress passes a crime bill that shunts $255 million to the INS for 1995, $181 million earmarked for border control, which is to include seven hundred new partners for the men who stopped Gus and me in our travels, and the history professor, and my friend's father, and as many as they could from South Tucson.

It is no use; borders haven't worked, and they won't work, not now, as the indigenous people of the Americas reassert their kinship and solidarity with one another. A mass migration is already under way; its roots are not simply economic. The Uto-Aztecan languages are spoken as far north as Taos Pueblo near the Colorado border, all the way south to Mexico City. Before the arrival of the Europeans, the indigenous communities throughout this region not only conducted commerce; the people shared cosmologies, and oral narratives about the Maize Mother, the Twin Brothers, and their grandmother, Spider Woman, as well as Quetzalcoatl, the benevolent snake. The great human migration within the Americas cannot be stopped; human beings are natural forces of the earth, just as rivers and winds are natural forces.

Deep down the issue is simple: the so-called Indian Wars from the days of Sitting Bull and Red Cloud have never really ended in the Americas. The Indian people of southern Mexico, of Guatemala, and those left in El Salvador, too, are still fighting for their lives and for their land against the cavalry patrols sent out by the governments of those lands. The Americas are Indian country, and the "Indian problem" is not about to go away.

One evening at sundown, we were stopped in traffic at a railroad crossing in downtown Tucson while a freight train passed us, slowly gaining speed as it headed north to Phoenix. In the twilight I saw the most amazing sight: dozens of human beings, mostly young men, were riding the train; everywhere, on flatcars, inside open boxcars, perched on top of boxcars, hanging off ladders on tank cars and between boxcars. I couldn't count fast enough, but I saw fifty or sixty people headed north. They were dark young men, Indian and mestizo; they were smiling and a few of them waved at us in our cars. I was reminded of the ancient story of Aztlán, told by the Aztecs but known in other Uto-Aztecan communities as well. Aztlán is the beautiful land to the north, the origin place of the Aztec people. I don't remember how or why the people left Aztlán to journey farther south, but the old story says that one day, they will return.

Fifth World: The Return of Ma ah shra true ee, the Giant Serpent

THE OLD-TIME people always told us kids to be patient, to wait, and then finally, after a long time, what you wish to know will become clear. The Pueblos and their paleo-Indian ancestors have lived continuously in the southwest of North America for twelve thousand years. So when the old-time people speak about "time" or "a long time," they're not speaking about a decade, or even a single lifetime; they can mean hundreds of years. And as the elders point out, the Europeans have hardly been on the continents of the Americas five hundred years. Still, they say, the longer Europeans or others live on these continents, the more they will become part of the Americas. The gravity of the continent under their feet begins this connection, which grows slowly in each generation. The process requires not hundreds, but thousands of years.

The prophecies foretelling the arrival of the Europeans to the Americas also say that over this long time, all things European will eventually disappear. The prophecies do not say the European people themselves will disappear, only their customs. The old people say that this has already begun to happen, and that it is a spiritual process that no armies will be able to stop. So the old people laugh when they hear talk about the "desecration" of the earth, because humankind, they know, is nothing in comparison to the earth. Blast it open, dig it up, or cook it with nuclear explosions: the earth remains. Humans desecrate only themselves. The earth is inviolate.

Tse'itsi'nako, Thought Woman,
is sitting in her room
and whatever she thinks about
appears.

She thought of her sisters,
Nau'ts'ity'i and I'tcts'ity'i,
and together they created the Universe
this world
and the four worlds below.

Thought Woman, the spider,
named things and
as she named them
they appeared.

She is sitting in her room
thinking of a story now

I'm telling you the story
she is thinking.

So perhaps it did not seem extraordinary to the old people that a giant stone snake formation was found one morning in the spring of 1980 by two employees of the Jackpile uranium mine. The mine is located near Paguate, one of seven villages in the Laguna Pueblo reservation in New Mexico. The employees, both Laguna Pueblo men, had been making a routine check of the mine when they discovered the biomorphic configuration near the base of mountainous piles of uranium tailings. The head of the snake was pointed west, its jaws open wide. The stone snake seemed to have always been there. The entire formation was more than thirty feet long and twelve inches high, an eccentric outcrop of yellow sandstone mottled and peppered with darker iron ores, like the stone that had once formed the mesas that had been swallowed up by the open-pit mine.

Reports of the snake formation were at first met with skepticism. The miners must be joking. People from Paguate village and other Laguna Pueblo people had hunted rabbits and herded sheep in that area for hundreds of years. Over time, wind and rain might uncover rock, but the process required years, not weeks. In any case, Laguna Pueblo people have a name and a story for every oddly-shaped boulder within two hundred miles—no way could anything like this giant stone snake have escaped notice. The mine employees swore they had walked the same route twice each month for inspections and seen nothing, and then suddenly, one morning the stone snake was there, uncoiling about three hundred yards from a Jackpile Mine truck yard. And soon there was a great deal of excitement among Pueblo religious people because the old stories mention a giant snake who is a messenger for the Mother Creator.

Ma ah shra true ee is the giant serpent
the sacred messenger spirit
from the Fourth World below.
He came to live at the Beautiful Lake, Kawaik,
that was once near Laguna village.
But neighbors got jealous.
They came one night and broke open the lake
so all the water was lost. The giant snake
went away after that. He has never been seen since.
That was the great misfortune for us, the Kawaik'meh,
at Old Laguna.

Before the days of the mining companies, the people of Paguate village had fields of corn and melons and beans scattered throughout the little flood plains below the yellow sandstone mesas southeast of the village. Apple and apricot orchards flourished there too. It was all dry farming in those days, dependent on prayers and ceremonies to call in the rain clouds. Back then, it was a different world, although ancient stories also recount terrible droughts and famines—times of great devastation. When large uranium deposits were discovered only a few miles southeast of Paguate village in the late 1940s, the Laguna Pueblo elders declared the earth was the sacred mother of all living things, and blasting her wide open to reach deposits of uranium ore was an act almost beyond imagination. But the advent of the Cold War had made the mining a matter of national security, and the ore deposits at the Jackpile Mine were vast and rich. As wards of the federal government, the small Pueblo tribe could not prevent the mining of their land. Now, the orchards and fields of melons are gone. Nearly all the land to the east and south of Paguate village has been swallowed by the mine; its open pit gapes within two hundred yards of the village.

Before world uranium prices fell, the mining companies

had proposed relocating the entire village to a new site a few miles away because the richest ore deposits lay directly under the old village. The Paguate people refused to trade their old houses for new all-electric ones; they were bound to refuse, because there is a small mossy spring that bubbles out of the base of a black lava formation on the west side of Paguate village. This spring is the Emergence Place, the entrance humans and animals used when they first climbed into this, the Fifth World. But the mining companies were not to be stopped; when they couldn't move the people, they simply sank shafts under the village.

When the mining began, the village elders and traditionalists maintained that no one of their people should work at the mine and participate in the sacrilege. But the early 1950s were drought years, and the Laguna people, who had struggled to live off their fields and herds, found themselves in trouble. Moreover, World War II and the Korean War had ushered in other changes within the community itself. The men who returned from military service had seen the world outside. They had worked for wages in the army, and when they came home to Laguna, they wanted jobs. Consequently, increasing numbers of Laguna men, and later women, began working the mine. Cranky old traditionalists predicted dire results from this desecration of the earth, but they had never been very specific about the terrible consequences. Meanwhile, Laguna Pueblo became one of the few reservations in the United States to enjoy nearly full employment. Twenty-five years passed, and then something strange and very sad began to happen at Paguate village.

"Tonight we'll see
if you really have magical power," they told him.

So that night
Pa'caya'nyi

came with his mountain lion.
He undressed
he painted his body
the whorls of flesh
the soles of his feet
the palms of his hands
the top of his head.

He wore feathers
on each side of his head.

He made an altar
with cactus spines
and purple locoweed flowers.
He lighted four cactus torches
at each corner.
He made the mountain lion lie
down in front and
then he was ready for his magic.

He struck the middle of the north wall.
He took a piece of flint and
he struck the middle of the north wall
and flowed down
toward the south.
He said, "What does that look like?
Is that magic powers?"
He struck the middle of the west wall
and from the east wall
a bear came out.
"What do you call this?"
he said again.

"Yes, it looks like magic all right,"
Ma'see'wi said.
So it was finished

and Ma'see'wi and Ou'yu'ye'wi
and all the people were fooled by
that Ck'o'yo medicine man,
Pa'caya'nyi.

From that time on
they were
so busy
playing around with that
Ck'o'yo magic
they neglected the Mother Corn altar.

They thought they didn't have to worry
about anything.

Pueblo communal systems value cooperation and nonaggression above all else. All problems, including the most serious, are resolved through negotiation by the families or clans of the aggrieved parties. Perhaps the harshness of the high desert plateau with its freezing winters and fierce summer droughts has had something to do with the supreme value the old people place upon cooperation and conciliation. For where margin for error is slender—even during the wet years—a seemingly trivial feud might hinder the mobilization and organization necessary to protect crops threatened by dramatic conditions of nature. Moreover, this system of cooperation extends to all living things, even plants and insects, which Laguna Pueblo elders refer to as sisters and brothers, because none can survive unless all survive.

Given this emphasis on balance and harmony, it was especially painful and confusing when, in 1973, Paguate became one of the first American communities to cope with the unexpected tragedy of a teenage suicide pact. The boys and girls all had attended Laguna-Acoma High School, and all but one of the suicides lived at Paguate. Some left suicide notes that made reference to an agreement the young people had made secretly. "Cherylyn did it Saturday so now it's my turn," for example, was the way the suicide notes read.

The Laguna people had already suffered suicides by army veterans sick with alcohol. But the suicide victims at Paguate had been the brightest and most promising students at the school. The usual psychological explanations—unstable family environment, absence of one parent, alienation—don't seem to apply here, as not one of the students had come from a poor or troubled family, and in fact, most had grown up in the house inhabited by their families for hundreds of years and were surrounded by supportive groups of relatives. While teachers and families tried in vain to learn more about the suicide club, it eventually claimed seven lives.

While suicide took its toll, the Pueblo community was disrupted by another horror, an apparently motiveless murder. A Saturday night party in Paguate turned into a slaughter. Two young men were hacked to death at the kitchen table by their friend, who had invited them to stop by the party after they got off swing shift at the mine. The killer then bullied another friend to drive a car they "borrowed," and while the friend drove around the reservation, the killer randomly dumped body parts in the weeds along the way. The impulse to pick up the shiny new axe had been irresistible, the killer later said. He could not explain the murder of his two friends.

But the old people have their own explanation. According to the elders, destruction of any part of the earth does immediate harm to all living things. Teachers at Indian School would ridicule these ideas; they would laugh and say, "How stupid you Indians are! How can the death of one tree in the jungle possibly affect a person in New York City!" But isn't it far more obvious these days *how* important that single tree in the rain forest of Brazil really is to the Manhattanite? And in the same way, the mesas of sandstone seemingly devoured by the uranium mine are as important, as essential. If it has taken environmental catastrophe to reveal to us why we need the rain forest, perhaps we might spare ourselves some tragedy by listening to the message of sand and stone in the form of a giant snake. Perhaps comprehension need not come from obvious catastrophes, like the destruction of the ozone layer, but more through subtle indications, like a stone snake come to remind us that violence in the Americas—against ourselves and against one another—can run as deep, but only as deep, as the deepest shafts with which humankind has pierced the earth.

WHEN I SAW the stone snake in June of 1980, I could hear the clanking and creaking of giant earthmovers on the other side of the mounds of tailings. The Jackpile Mine generators roared continuously night and day, seven days a week. At noon, when Jackpile did the blasting, everyone made sure to be indoors because potato-size rocks frequently landed on Paguate doorsteps. (These were the normal, day-to-day living conditions of the Laguna Pueblos in and around Paguate for many years.) Old barbed wire had been loosely strung along a few makeshift juniper posts until someone provided a sagging barrier of chain-link fencing, intended to protect the stone snake from livestock and photographers. Corn meal and pollen, bits of red coral and turquoise had been sprinkled over the snake's head as offerings of spirit food. Holy people from tribes as far away as Canada and Mexico had come to see the giant snake.

There have been attempts to confine the meaning of the

snake to an official story suitable for general consumption. But the Laguna Pueblos go on producing their own rich and continuously developing body of oral and occasionally written stories that reject any decisive conclusion in favor of ever-increasing possibilities. This production of multiple meaning is in keeping with Pueblo cosmology in general. For the old people, no one person or thing is better than another; hierarchies presuming superiority and inferiority are considered absurd. No thing or location on the earth is of greater or lesser value than another. And this means that any location can potentially become a sacred spot.

Thus, outsiders who visit the American southwest are often confused by the places in which they find sacred altars or sites of miraculous appearances of the Blessed Virgin or others (could it be the notion of original sin that causes Europeans to define the sacred as the virginal or pure?). They expect to find the *milagros* of Nuestra Señora de Guadalupe in pristine forest grottoes, *not* on the window glass of a cinder block school building in a Yaqui Indian town; or Jesus' face in a rainbow above Yosemite Falls, not on a poor New Mexican woman's breakfast tortilla. The traditional notion of the wondrous in a splendid setting befitting its claim is subverted here in this landscape where the wondrous can be anywhere and is everywhere. Even in the midst of a strip-mining operation.

Just as the Laguna prophecies say that all things European will eventually pass away, Europeans have, particularly in the last century, predicted the demise of all things Native American. In the late 1960s, anthropologists lugged their tape recorders to the pueblos, so that they might have the elders record stories and songs that would be lost when they passed away. Most of the Laguna elders agreed to make the tape recordings, but a few of the old people took a hard line.

They said that what is important to our children and our grandchildren will be remembered; what is forgotten is what is no longer meaningful. What is true will persist. In spite of everything, Ma ah shra true ee, the sacred messenger, will appear again and again. Nothing can stop that. Not even a uranium mine.

The wind stirred the dust.
The people were starving.
"She's angry with us,"
the people said.
"Maybe because of that
Ck'o'yo magic
we were fooling with.
We better send someone
to ask our forgiveness."

They noticed hummingbird
was fat and shiny
he had plenty to eat.
They asked how come he
looked so good.

He said
Down below
Three worlds below this one
everything is
green
all the plants are growing
the flowers are blooming
I go down there
and eat.

Notes on *Almanac of the Dead*

I WORK BY intuition and instinct; I don't make outlines or plans because whenever I do, they turn out to be useless. It is as if I am compelled to violate the scope of any outline or plan; it is as if the writing does not want me to know what is about to happen. In 1980, I became interested in the work of certain archaeologists who were studying the ancient astronomical observatories and the astronomical knowledge that the tribal people of the Americas had possessed long before the arrival of the Europeans. I read about the great culture of the Maya people, who had invented the zero and who had performed sophisticated mathematical calculations so that they could predict the positions of the planets and the stars.

What interested me about the Mayas was their notion of time; they believed time was a living being that had a personality, a sort of identity. Time was alive and might pass, but time did not die; moreover, the days and weeks eventually would return.

Since the days eventually returned, the Maya believed it was possible to know the future, if one understood the identities, or souls, of the days from their last appearance among humans. Certain people in touch with the spirits knew the days, weeks, months, and years intimately and could say exactly whether the days to come were peaceful, full of plenty, or menacing and on the brink of disaster. The Maya people kept track of the days, and weeks, and months, and years in extensive almanacs.

The Maya people made beautiful paper, and they had libraries as the Aztec people had libraries, but Bishop Landa and the Spaniards burned hundreds of thousands of the books. Fragments remain of only three of the Maya almanacs; they are all incomplete. The codices, as they are called, are named for the cities where the fragments were located: Madrid, Dresden, and Paris.

I have always been interested in theories of time other than linear time. I don't understand it very well, but I find the theory of curvature in space-time very exciting, and I also love what happens to time when subatomic particles begin bouncing off one another. I love how these particles signal one another or "know" at a speed faster than that of light.

My interest in time comes from my childhood with the old-time people, who had radically different views of the universe and reality. For the old-time people, time was not a series of ticks of a clock, one following the other. For the old-time people, time was round—like a tortilla; time had specific moments and specific locations, so that the beloved ancestors who had passed on were not annihilated by death, but only relocated to the place called Cliff House. At Cliff House, people continued as they had always been, although only spirits and not living humans can travel freely over this tortilla of time. All times go on existing side by side for all eternity. No moment is lost or destroyed. There are no future times or past times; there are *always all* the times, which differ slightly, as the locations on the tortilla differ slightly. The past and the future are the same because they exist only in the present of our imaginations. We can think and speak only in the present, but as we do it is becoming the past, which is always present and which always contains the future encoded in it. Without clocks or calendars we see only the succession of the days, some longer, some shorter, some hotter, some colder; but the succession is cyclic. Without calendars and clocks, the process of aging becomes a process of changing: the infant changes; the flower changes; the changes continue relentlessly. Nothing is lost, left behind, or destroyed. It is only changed.

I began thinking about the ancient Maya almanacs and how they had predicted down to the exact day the arrival of Cortes. Modern scientists who are envious of ancient Maya mathematicians call their accurate prediction of the European arrival a coincidence. I already knew that among the tribal people there were those who could see what was happening great distances away.

All the Native American tribes have prophecies that predicted the invasion by the Europeans; but the prophecies also say that all things European will gradually disappear from the Americas.

Around this same time, I was visiting a neighbor when he received a phone call intended for another party. The caller had been seeking a psychic who had appeared on a television talk show in Atlanta. The caller was desperately trying to contact the TV psychic, but all she had was the psychic's name and Tucson as the location. Right then, I started to imagine what it might be like to be a psychic who took long-distance phone calls all day, listening to frantic parents and loved ones searching for the disappeared. I think I began to imagine a young woman who had lost her young child and who might seek the aid of a psychic she had seen on TV.

Later on, I thought this psychic might know how to converse with snakes, because I had been thinking a lot about the old-time Pueblo beliefs concerning snakes, especially rattlesnakes. I'd moved to Tucson from Laguna in 1978 and at my place in the Tucson Mountains I had seen a number of large rattlesnakes that had seemed extremely gentle and tame—probably because no one had been killing them and they had forgotten how bad people were. Or maybe I was thinking about snakes because I was homesick for the way people at Laguna see everything as being related; they like to say someone is related to the coyotes or that a snake looks like someone's uncle. Anyway, I had been able to approach and talk to the rattlesnakes that I encountered in the Tucson Mountains, and they had not coiled or rattled, and a couple of the snakes had even seemed curious about me. I started to think about what the old-time people at Laguna used to say about the snakes. I tried to recall the old-time stories I'd heard that had comments about snakes.

Then in 1979, while I was at Laguna looking for locations for the filming of the Estoymuut movie, I heard about the giant stone snake that had appeared near the Jackpile uranium mine. I went and saw the snake, which had by then become a religious shrine (it is off limits now to the public). The giant stone snake seemed a great mystery to me, although I knew that the traditional Pueblo medicine people knew its meaning. Rumors circulated around Laguna about the meaning of the appearance of the snake. I made the Estoymuut movie and went back to Tucson and I never quite forgot about the stone snake I'd seen. One rumor said it was a sign that the uranium mine and the people who depended on it and things of its ilk had won, and the snake was pointing at the next mesa the open pit would devour. But the next thing I heard was that the Jackpile Mine had closed because of a worldwide uranium glut; that meant the rumor about the mine winning had been wrong. Laguna always has rumors abounding, and most of them wildly exaggerated. It was a relief to think maybe the mine and all that it symbolizes had not yet won.

But in 1981, when I began writing notes and actual sections of what became *Almanac of the Dead,* I began to notice the criminality that seemed to permeate Tucson. It seemed very ancient and very fierce, and I began to read the history of the border and northern Sonora from the time of the Portuguese monster de Guzman, the slave catcher in the 1500s, to the present. I did more reading about the Apache wars and about Geronimo, who had been betrayed and sent to prison forever from Tucson. I read that John Dillinger had been illegally extradited from Tucson to Indiana, and I began to wonder if there was something in the very bedrock, in the very depths of the earth beneath Tucson, that caused such treachery, such greed and cruelty.

I began to have vivid dreams. Early one morning, I dreamed U.S. Army helicopters were flying out of the south. I saw them flying low over saguaro cactus forests with their doors wide open. They flew low enough in my dream that I could look inside the helicopter doors. I saw dead and wounded U.S. soldiers. I knew they had died in a war in Mexico, and that Tucson had become like Saigon in the days of the Vietnam War.

Nineteen eighty-one was the year I was awarded the

five-year writing fellowship by the John D. and Catherine T. MacArthur Foundation. I was still reading and making notes; I knew I wanted to start a new novel, but when the MacArthur Prize Fellowship came, I spent the first year finishing the Estoymuut movie. During that year, I was always getting ideas out of the blue and having to take notes while I was at a bar or while I was driving or talking to someone. I knew Geronimo would be in the novel. I knew I would have a psychic and there would be drug smugglers and corrupt government officials. By the end of 1981, I was working on sections that I hoped would fit together much as the old Maya almanacs had fit together. I already knew I would call this book *Almanac of the Dead* and that in the book somehow the characters would foretell the future.

By 1982, I was writing the novel in sections, much as a movie is filmed for later editing; the sections also resembled the fragments that remained of the ancient Maya codices. I wrote the novel in these sections because I could not think of the story of the *Almanac* as a single line moving from point A to point B to point C. I knew that I wanted to shape time inside my *Almanac.* I wanted to use narrative to shift the reader's experience of time and the meaning of history as stories that mark certain points in time (when time is a long string of markers or points on the pages of a calendar). I had to figure out how to do this and still tell stories people could understand. Myths alter our experience of time and reality without disappointing our desire for a story. I knew *Almanac of the Dead* must be made of myths—all sorts of myths from the Americas, including the modern myths.

In 1983, I made a small clay figure inspired by the giant stone snake that had appeared near the uranium mine. I also made photographs and copier prints from photographs of big inflatable snakes floating among the water lilies in my pool. I'm good friends with the snakes that live in the vicinity of my house; I suspect a rattlesnake hibernates each winter under the floor near the kitchen sink. My ranch house was built in 1929, and all the desert creatures have some access. Of course I knew my interest in snakes had been increased since the discovery of the giant stone snake near the mine.

On Good Friday, I came across a strange front-page article about a dead parachutist who later turned out to be a navy SEAL killed in a secret training mission. Why would a SEAL need to know how to parachute into the Sonoran desert? A few weeks later, a short article in *New York* magazine quoted an army general at Fort Huachuca, south of Tucson. The general had claimed there was a leftist threat from the south: "Today Tegucigalpa, tomorrow Tucson" was the title of the article.

By 1984, I felt ready to begin a rough draft of the *Almanac* using the sections and notes that I had been writing since 1981. I decided I had to find a workplace away from my house in order to complete the novel, so I rented space from a lawyer in an old building on Stone Avenue not far from downtown Tucson. The neighborhood turned out to be perfect for a novelist: late at night automatic rifle fire used to break out in the parking lots of nearby motel lounges. In the fall, homeless people arrived with their kids and wives on freight trains and in broken-down cars from all over the United States; they were looking for work, and Stone Avenue was only three blocks from the Salvation Army. I saw the United States of America that no one wants to talk about. And from the lawyers who frequented the law office in the building, I began to hear many stories about the justice system in Pima County and southern Arizona.

In the fall of 1985, I began to feel nervous about finishing *Almanac* by the time the MacArthur Prize Fellowship ran out. The novel was over one thousand pages in manuscript by then, but I still felt I was only halfway, although I did not dare tell anyone the truth. My first novel, *Ceremony,* had been published in 1977, and naturally colleagues, friends, enemies, and family were all beginning to wonder. What did I do all day long locked in my office? I can remember a poet advising me that the second novel should be something short and simple in order to avoid the terrible jinx of "the second novel."

Why hadn't I taken the poet's advice?

What had I done to myself?

Worst of all, I had already spent four precious years of my MacArthur Fellowship on this book and it wasn't anywhere near finished. But I was completely captivated by my characters and by the *Almanac* by then. I was getting ideas and inspirations constantly and having to write them down; that's how the novel kept getting bigger and bigger. The scenes, the actions, the bits of dialogue just kept pouring into my head. Even if I had wanted to, I knew I would not be able to write anything else until I finished writing about these characters and places.

Still, I can remember that by the fall of 1986 I was still not sure how the novel would end or even if I could get control of these characters and force them to move toward an end.

Because I needed money and because I wanted to force myself to finish *Almanac,* I asked my agent to try to sell the novel on the basis of the first 660 pages. With the novel sold, I knew I would have deadlines, and I hoped the deadlines would help me get control over my characters who were taking me all over North, Central, and South America in the course of about five hundred years.

At this time, Arizona politics outraged me enough that I took a can of spray paint outside and painted graffiti on the wall of a building visible from Stone Avenue. *Recall Mechem. Impeach him. Indict him. Eat more politicians, end war, end taxes.* My landlord, the lawyer, let the graffiti stay on the wall until Mechem was recalled. After the wall had been whitewashed, I decided to paint something nice for the people of the neighborhood, who had endured the graffiti.

The urge to paint the wall became stronger than the urge to sit at my typewriter and wrestle with the new characters who had appeared, Mexican Indians from the Maya country. I decided I would paint and just let the novel sit for a few weeks.

I don't know why, maybe because the wall was so long, but I walked outside one day with my paint and I outlined the figure of a rattlesnake thirty feet long. I liked the snake so much that I didn't want to stop with just the snake figure. I kept painting. The longer I worked on the mural, the better I felt about the novel. I worked some days on the novel, other days painting my mural, which eventually measured forty by twelve feet. As the mural began to work out beautifully, I realized it was somehow a sign to me that the novel would work out also, and I would be able to complete it successfully.

At that time, although I had the giant stone snake in *Almanac,* and I had made the connection between the giant snake deities of the Americas and of Africa, I still did not realize fully the meaning of the giant snake. After I had painted the mural, though, I felt as if the giant snake was somehow involved with the end of the novel, but I didn't know how.

Gradually, in 1988, I began to realize the relationship between the mural of the snake and the latter part of my novel. The snake in my mural is a messenger. He emerges out of a rainstorm and is surrounded by flowers, birds, and other creatures. His belly is full of skulls. Above the snake I painted words in Spanish as if they had blossomed out of the flowers and plants that grew around the giant snake. The words are in Spanish and this is what they say: "The people are hungry. The people are cold. The rich have stolen the land. The rich have stolen freedom. The people demand justice. Otherwise, Revolution."

But it wasn't until mid-1989, when I wrote the last sentence of *Almanac,* that I realized that the giant snake had been a catalyst for the novel from the start. In a way, one might almost say that I had to write this novel in order to figure out for myself the meaning of the giant stone snake that had appeared near the uranium mine in 1979.

I never thought the novel would take ten years to write. Acquaintances and even friends dropped away over those years because I no longer wrote letters or returned their phone calls. How could I? I was a prisoner of my characters, who each day left me drained of all emotion and thought until I could barely interact with a clerk at the supermarket checkout counter.

After years of playing the devoted daughter and sister, I had flaked out on my family; since my sons know me only as a writer, they didn't see much difference. But rumors fly; people speculate about what has happened to you. After the fifth or sixth year, colleagues and acquaintances begin to get uncomfortable when you tell them the novel is almost finished. They no longer conceal their doubts; sometimes they are sarcastic or condescending. Friends and family become concerned and then disappointed and angry. I couldn't blame them; by that time I really had spent so much time with my characters that they had in a way replaced real human beings. Everyday human beings weren't nearly as exciting and interesting as my characters, either.

Now that the novel is finished, I will have to begin trying to reintegrate myself into the real world; I will have to see if I have any friends remaining.

Tribal Prophecies

NATIVE AMERICAN TRIBES have ancient prophecies that have been retold for thousands of years, generation upon generation. All the prophecies foretell the invasion by the Europeans. The Maya and Aztec almanacs predicted the arrival of Cortes to the day, 11 Ahau (Maya reckoning). No one here was surprised when the Europeans showed up. Only the cruelty of the Europeans astonished the people. The invaders had set fire to the groves of the sacred macaws and parrots, and hundreds of the sacred birds had been burned alive.

Maybe the tribal sorcerers of the Americas, already familiar with evil themselves, had conjured up more evil by calling out these white men from Europe, their spiritual brethren in destruction and suffering. The Europeans arrived fresh from the church Inquisition against "all heretics," which had legitimized torture and death in the name of the Holy Catholic Church. Torture and death have been the centerpieces of Christianity in the Americas from the beginning. Seventy million people throughout the Americas died in the first one hundred years, from 1520 to 1620. Hundreds of years before the German Nazis fashioned lamp shades out of Jewish skin, the Portuguese slave hunter, de Guzman, made lamp shades from the skins of Native Americans.

The ancient prophecies not only foretell the invasion by the Europeans. The prophecies predict bullets and aircrafts, describing small deadly objects that fly through the air, and flying objects that people could ride. The prophecies predict great turmoil and suffering; natural catastrophes that destroy millions of lives. They predict terrible droughts and famines, the disappearance of the animals. Then, after a long time, all things European will gradually disappear, and the rain will return, and the animals will come back, and the herds of buffalo on the great plains. The tribal people of the Americas, like the tribal people of Africa, will regain their ancestral lands.

The gentle giant, Quetzalcoatl, Divine Serpent of Feathers and Flowers, was savagely attacked by the European church and labeled Satan. But in the Americas and in Africa, the people loved and worshipped the gentle giant Damballah, or Quetzalcoatl, or Ma ah shra true ee, Divine Snake of the Beautiful Lake. Maybe the Old Testament garden of Eden story is the first strike by northern tribes against the religion of the Africans to the south and their worship of the great snake, Damballah. Those who loathe snakes have been brainwashed by the Old Testament. Even ordinary snakes are spirit messengers to the spirit beings and Mother Earth.

Now a giant stone snake has appeared, a messenger from the spirit world, announcing the changes to come. The stone snake looks to the south as if he is waiting for someone to appear. The people. Thousands upon thousands, and later millions, all walk north.

Stone Avenue Mural

La gente tiene hambre. La gente tiene frío.
Los ricos han robado la tierra.
Los ricos han robado la libertad.
La gente exige justicia. De otra manera, Revolución.

The people are hungry. The people are cold.
The rich have stolen the land.
The rich have stolen freedom.
The people demand justice. Otherwise, Revolution.

. . . This is no new war. This war has a five-hundred-year history. This is the same war of resistance that the indigenous

people of the Americas have never ceased to fight . . . We are all part of the old stories. Whether we know the stories or not, the stories know about us. From time immemorial, the old stories encompass all events, past and future. The spirits of the ancestors cry out for justice. Their voices are louder now. The mountains shake and fall; the hurricane winds scour the earth; fire and flood engulf the cities as the ancestor spirits announce the time that will return.

Human beings also are natural forces of the earth. There will be no peace in the Americas until there is justice for the earth and her children.

Painted in 1986–1987, the mural is located at 930 North Stone Avenue, Tucson, Arizona; it is approximately 12' x 36' long, acrylic on unprimed brick.

An Expression of Profound Gratitude to the Maya Zapatistas, January 1, 1994

WHEN I WAS a child at Kawaik, in the Laguna Pueblo reservation in New Mexico, the old folks used to tell us to listen and to remember the stories that tell us who we are as a people. The old folks said the stories themselves had the power to protect us and even to heal us because the stories are alive; the stories are our ancestors. In the very telling of the stories, the spirits of our beloved ancestors and family become present with us. The ancestors love us and care for us though we may not know this.

The stories I heard as a child told us about another time, when all of Mother Earth's children, the birds, lizards, bugs, plants, and human beings, lived together as one family. They shared the water and the food equally; they behaved justly with one another. The time and place of this harmony and justice still exists; it is not gone or destroyed. Greed blinds human eyes to the location of this place and time nearby to us.

From the beginning there have always been those destroyers who delight in the suffering and destruction of Mother Earth and her children. These destroyers are liars, of course, and they want the people to lose heart; so the destroyers always tell the people that the old stories are ended, the old stories don't matter anymore. But the truth is, the stories don't ever end; they continue on; the old stories continue to unfold even now, in many locations, not just in Chiapas with the Maya Zapatistas.

From the Antarctic to the Arctic, all the indigenous communities of the Americas have ancient stories that foretold the invasion of the Americas by the Europeans; the old stories prophesied the suffering and destruction that the people of the Americas would endure. The old stories even foretold the amazing high technologies humans would someday possess. But the old stories also tell of another time, when all things incompatible with Mother Earth will disappear and all those who attached themselves to such things will also disappear.

The intrepid Maya people of Chiapas know very well the story, the history that they are living as they rise up against the genocidal policies of the Mexican government, tool of the greedy profiteers who violate Mother Earth and poison her children. This is no new war; this war has a five-hundred-year history; this is the same war of resistance that the indigenous people of the Americas have never ceased to fight.

We are all part of the old stories; whether we know the

stories or not, the old stories know about us. From time immemorial the old stories encompass all events, past and future. The spirits of the ancestors cry out for justice. Their voices are louder now. The mountains shake and fall; the hurricane winds scour the earth; fire and flood engulf the cities as the ancestor spirits announce the time will return. Human beings also are natural forces of the earth. There will be no peace in the Americas until there is justice for the earth and her children.

Books: Notes on Mixtec and Maya Screenfolds, Picture Books of Preconquest Mexico

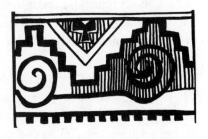

Books were and still are weapons in the ongoing struggle for the Americas. Only a few years ago, a best-selling novelist breathed new life into old racist stereotypes with a portrayal of the Cherokee reservation people as pitiful drunks and child abusers whose children are better off with any white woman who comes along. Such sentiments soothe the collective conscience of white America. The subtext of such stereotypical portrayals is: Take the children, take the land; these Indians are in no condition to have such precious possessions.

Codex refers to European illuminated manuscripts consisting of pages bound on one side. The Nuttal painted book and the other surviving picture books from preconquest southern Mexico, as well as three surviving Maya preconquest manuscripts (Dresden, Madrid, Paris), are actually screenfolds of animal skin or *amatl,* agave bark paper. The animal skin or paper was covered with a thin coat of lime plaster, on which was painted in various colors (jade green, ochre yellow, black, white, light red, and medium red), encased in black outlines, the images of the picture book.

The screenfolds, complementing non-Western, nonlinear thought, store information so that several pages may be viewed simultaneously. When folded out, the screenfold served as a mural.

Sixteenth-century Spaniards called the books paintings. They were painted by *tlacuilos* (a Nahuatl term meaning painter and scribe). Pictographs depicted objects in a stylized manner. Ideographs conveyed qualities and categories associated with the object presented. Phonetic symbols, which were still few, indicate names of places, people, or dates. The written language functioned as a sort of rebus. *Cuetzalli* (red quetzal feathers) and *tlantli* (tooth) equals place name *Cuetzalan,* written as four feathers over a tooth.

The writing must be read like a painting, that is, the colors and lines and figures within give the reader the clue of how to read the painting, which area was meant to be read first, and so forth. Sometimes red lines indicated the directions. Page layout, the scale of the symbols, the position they occupy in relation to one another, and the way they are grouped together are all elements that determine which direction the writing is to be read and its ultimate meaning. The colors filling the spaces made by these regular strokes constituted chromatic variations, which influence meaning.

The Mixtec and Maya combined painting and writing, two activities that European culture considers distinct. People probably talked about the images as the books were unfolded, so that while the eye scanned the images, the ear heard the words of the narrative. Both concrete and abstract ideas could be expressed in picture writing.

For the people, these images were more than images are for Europeans. Certain aspects of the divine world were actually present, at least for a while, in these images. Thus the people ritually fed the books with sacrificial blood. The universe of the gods came to life through the coupling of the brush to the bark paper. The Spaniards noticed this devotion to the paintings, and beginning in 1520, the book burning by the missionaries and colonialists began.

Eight Mixtec histories from Oaxaca remain.

Six ritual books, the Borgia group, remain.

Three Maya books remain: in Dresden, Paris, and Madrid.

In 1540, the great libraries of the Americas were burned by the European invaders, most of whom were illiterate but not stupid. They burned the great libraries because they wished to foster the notion that the New World was populated by savages. Savages could be slaughtered and enslaved; savages were no better than wild beasts and thus had no property rights. International law regulated the fate of conquered nations but not of savages or beasts.

Eight Mixtec screenfold books are known to have survived the fires of the invaders: the Codex Nuttal; the Codices Bodley and Selden, which are at the Bodleian Library at Oxford; the reverse of the Codex Vienna; the Codex Columbino, located at the *museo* in Mexico City; the Codices Becker I and II in Vienna; and the Codex Sanchez Solis in the British Museum. There are also six ritual books in the painted-picture screenfold style, which are most likely Mixtec, and they are referred to as the Borgia group. Codex Borgia is in the Vatican library; the Codex Laud, in the Bodleian Library at Oxford; the Codex Fejervary-Mayer, at the Liverpool Free Public Museum; the Codex Cospi, in the University Library, Bologna; the Codex Vaticanus B, in the Vatican; and the Mexican Manuscript #20, in the Bibliothèque Nationale in Paris.

There are three known surviving Maya screenfold books: the Codex Dresden, the Codex Madrid, and the Codex Paris. They are named for the cities where they are now kept. Of course, those two old Yaqui women in my novel *Almanac of the Dead* possess large portions of a fourth Maya book, which survived the five-hundred-year war for the Americas. Recently this old almanac of theirs correctly predicted the Zapatista uprising. Their old almanac even purports to explain the unfortunate assassination of Señor Colosio in Tijuana.

Books have always been important for my family. As a child I remember the old lament the family had about the signed first edition of *Ben-Hur* that had disappeared. Local legend had it that Lew Wallace had written a portion of *Ben-Hur* in the priests' quarters at the mission church. I never heard what brought the novel-writing territorial governor of New Mexico to the Laguna's San Jose Mission. Maybe he needed to escape the mad social whirl of Santa Fe in order to finish his novel. Maybe he was a friend or relative of one of the Franciscan priests at the mission.

My great-grandmother's house had a tall bookcase full of my great-grandfather's books. My grandparents' house also had rooms with shelves of books. We had books. My parents kept books at their bedsides. My father used to read at the table at lunchtime, and we did too. It was years before I realized it is considered impolite to read at the table. I remember waiting until I was alone in the house, and then I'd go find *Lolita* or *Lady Chatterley's Lover* half hidden under my dad's side of the bed.

I have a friend who grew up in a house without books. There was a Bible and there were cattle growers' magazines, but he was in the sixth or seventh grade before a cousin going off to war gave him the first books he ever owned. My friend still suffers with insatiable lust for books. While his father and uncles counted cattle, my friend counted his books. My friend couldn't tell one cow from another, but he knew how to spot the books he wanted whenever the high school basketball team took a trip to the big city.

The heyday of the cattle drives and open range didn't last long. Stampedes, storms, angry Indians, and bandits never did get to that great old cowboy Charles Goodnight, but lawyers and their books laid old Goodnight low. No wonder the cowboys distrusted books. They must have distrusted my friend too, when they sensed his passion for books. They clung to their old life, the old cowboy culture with its devotion to livestock and to the land long after the heyday of the cowboys had passed. These cowboys believed in action, not words, certainly not the printed word.

Hundreds of years before, proclamations, letters, and edicts came to the Americas from monarchs and popes admonishing the settlers to obey the laws. In the Americas, the printed word, like the spoken word, had to be ignored if the settlers were to reap the riches they all desired. If you could not read the king's or the pope's edict, then you could not be held accountable. If you were ignorant of the pope's edict then you were blameless before God. So illiteracy and the aversion to books that is found through the Americas descends from colonial times. Ignorance was blissful and profitable.

My great-grandmother and Aunt Susie had been sent

away to Carlisle Indian School in Pennsylvania, and both women had returned with a profound sense of the power of books. The laws were in books. The king of Spain had granted the Laguna Pueblo people their land. The Laguna Pueblo people knew their land was protected by a land grant document from the king of Spain. The Anglo-Americans who swarmed into the New Mexico Territory after 1848 carried with them no such documents. The Pueblo people fared better than other tribes simply because of these documents. The land grant documents alerted the Pueblo people to the value of the written word; the old books of international law favored the holders of royal land grants. So, very early, the Pueblo people realized the power of written words and books to secure legitimate title to tribal land. No wonder the older folks used to tell us kids to study: learn to read and to write for your own protection.

Grandma A'mooh used to read to me and my sisters over and over from a tattered little book called *Brownie the Bear.* My father and my uncles also remember *Brownie the Bear.* People told stories constantly, but Grandma A'mooh made a point of reading to us from a book too, perhaps because she feared we'd prefer listening to reading (who wouldn't?). But when I got to school and there were no beloved grandmas or aunts to tell me stories, I remembered that books tell stories too, and whenever I felt alienated and lonely in school, I would begin to read a story, and immediately I felt that happy secure feeling come over me as it did whenever Grandma A'mooh began telling me a story. I used to make up stories for my sisters and cousins because I learned very early that I got the same pleasure from telling stories as I felt when I was a listener.

Later, in fifth grade, I learned that when it was not possible to be soothed by hearing a story or by telling a story aloud, I could evoke that same feeling of well-being by writing down a story I made up myself. Fifth grade was when my sisters and I had to commute to Albuquerque to school, and I was very unhappy. Mrs. Cooper, the fifth-grade teacher, asked us to make up a story that used the words in our spelling list at least once. The spelling list had the word *poplar*, and I remember I had a character sliding down the smooth bark of the poplar tree. Of course I had no idea what a poplar tree looked like.

A book was the cause of the only big quarrel my great-grandmother ever had with her daughter-in-law Aunt Susie. The old-time Pueblo people abhorred confrontations, especially with family members. So I was almost grown and Grandma A'mooh had passed on before my mother ever discussed the incident. The quarrel had occurred years before, and few people knew about it; but Grandma A'mooh was very fond of my mother and told her the story.

It seems that when the War Department surveyed graduates of the Carlisle Indian School, they noted shocking recidivism; the graduates who had once looked so well scrubbed and earnest in their dark suits and long dresses "went back to the blanket" as soon as they returned home. They abandoned civilized clothing; they grew their hair long again, and they refused to speak English.

The U.S. government had taken every precaution to sever the Indian students' ties with their families and tribes. Children were taken by force, if necessary, put on the train, and sent thousands of miles to the boarding school in Carlisle, Pennsylvania. The government did not allow the children to return home for visits in the summer. Instead the Indian students were hired out to Carlisle families for domestic and farm work. The government policymakers believed that if the Indian children were kept far enough away from their families and homeland long enough, the Indian School graduates might never return to the reservations but instead melt into the cities in the east to work as maids and farmhands.

What was needed was an extension program that would reach Carlisle graduates after they returned home, to reinforce all of the civilizing and instruction given at the boarding school. Thus it was that the book *Stiya, The Story of an Indian Girl* came to be. Marion Bergess, a white woman who worked as a teacher and dormitory matron at Carlisle, wrote the novel under the fake Indian name Tonka. The U.S. War Department published the book in 1881; as far as I know, distribution was limited to Indian boarding school graduates.

The book was written from the point of view of a young Pueblo girl named Stiya after she has returned home from Carlisle and struggles to retain her new identity and "civilized" ways despite growing hostility and pressure from her family and from the Pueblo community where she grew up. Marion Bergess revealed the whites' perspective of Pueblo people as she described the sights and smells of the village, which repel Stiya and even nauseate her. Bergess projected all of her own fears and prejudices toward Pueblo life into her Stiya character. Stiya refuses to wear traditional Pueblo clothing and she speaks only English although her family absurdly insists she speak their "gibberish." She refuses to go to the plaza for the sacred *ka'tsina* dances because they are "lewd." Just when she seems most alone, when the pressure of the tribal elders seems almost to break her, the government arrests and imprisons those same elders for performing "obscene" pagan dances. Stiya is right and good; all the others are wrong, bad and dirty—very, very dirty. Bergess could not emphasize too much the filth and the odors she imagined in Stiya's village.

There are a number of authentic memoirs and autobiographies of Indian women who went away to Indian Boarding School around 1900. Helen Sekaquaptewa describes the experience in her book *Me and Mine: The Life Story of Helen Sekaquaptewa,* and Polingasi Qoyawayma (Elizabeth Q. White) also describes her experiences after returning from a government boarding school in her book *No Turning Back.* Although the readjustment to village life was not easy for these young Indian women, still the reader is struck by the overwhelming love and respect that the women have for their families and communities despite the numerous conflicts that did arise between the boarding school graduates and village traditionalists.

By contrast, the Stiya character Bergess created is detached from land and from village life. The Stiya character has no affection for any family member; every aspect of Pueblo life is repugnant; vile odors and flies abound. Stiya is filled with self-loathing when she remembers that she grew up in this place. She has only loathing for the traditional Pueblo ways. Stiya wonders how she can possibly endure the squalor, and these questions were exactly the sort that the U.S. Department of War wanted Indian School graduates to ask themselves. It was never too late for a Carlisle graduate to move to the city.

All Carlisle Indian School graduates who returned to their home reservations received a copy of *Stiya* in an attempt to inoculate them against their "uncivilized" families and communities. I don't know what year this was, but since Aunt Susie was already married to Uncle Walter, it must have been around 1900.

As soon as the parcels from Carlisle began to arrive at the post office, there must have been a stir of excitement among the Carlisle graduates. Those who had graduated some years before were quite curious about the book. Aunt Susie would have been one of the first to finish reading *Stiya* because she loved to read. Grandma A'mooh began reading the book but, as she read, she became increasingly incensed at the libelous portrayal of Pueblo life and people. There was a particularly mendacious passage concerning the Pueblo practice of drying meat in the sun. The meat was described as bloody and covered with flies. Grandma A'mooh was outraged.

About this time, Aunt Susie came over. Aunt Susie loved discussions and she was anxious to find out what Grandma thought about the book. But Grandma A'mooh was in no mood for discussion; she told Aunt Susie the only place for this book was in the fire, and she lifted the lid on her cookstove to drop in the book.

Aunt Susie was a scholar and a storyteller; she believed the *Stiya* book was important evidence of the lies and the racism and bad faith of the U.S. government with the Pueblo people. Grandma A'mooh didn't care about preserving historical evidence of racist, anti-Indian propaganda; a book's lies should be burned just as witchcraft paraphernalia is destroyed. Arguments and face-to-face confrontations between mother-in-law and daughter-in-law were avoided if possible, but that day they argued over a book.

Aunt Susie could not persuade my great-grandmother that the book should be spared for future Pueblo historians. So finally Aunt Susie said, "Well, if you are going to burn the book, then give it to me." According to Pueblo etiquette, it would have been unthinkable for my great-grandmother to refuse her daughter-in-law's request for the book, especially since my great-grandmother was about to destroy it. So Grandma A'mooh gave Aunt Susie her copy of the *Stiya* book, and our side of the family didn't have a copy of the notorious book. Years passed before I ever saw a copy of the book, in the rare book room of the University of New Mexico Library in Albuquerque.

Books like *Stiya,* purportedly written by Indians about Indian life, still outnumber books actually written by Indians. It is because of books like *Stiya* that Native American communities concern themselves with the origins and authorship of so-called Indian novels and Indian poetry. Books have been the focus of the struggle for the control of the Americas from the start. The great libraries of the Americas were destroyed in 1540 because the Spaniards feared the political and spiritual power of books authored by the indigenous people. As Vine Deloria has pointed out, non-Indians are still more comfortable with Indian books written by non-Indians than they are with books by Indian authors.

Now, fewer than five hundred years after the great libraries of the Americas were burned, a great blossoming of Native American writers is under way.

As a Child I Loved to Draw and Cut Paper

As a child, I loved to draw and cut paper and paste things together, although I was not as adept as my classmates and my work always looked messy next to theirs. But I didn't care that my projects looked crooked because I got such pleasure out of making things. I did the best that I could, and I had fun.

At the University of New Mexico, I wanted to major in visual arts, but I soon realized that years of looking at Pueblo pottery designs and Navajo weaving had made it unlikely that I would ever master the principles of visual perspective needed to make realistic drawings. So I stayed with literature and writing because stories and books were very important to me and my family, and writing had made a great deal of difference in my life since the fifth grade. Once I got started, I wrote effortlessly and I got A's. But I never have stopped drawing and painting, and I still love cutting and pasting paper.

After I dropped out of law school, in 1971, I enrolled in a beginning photography course. I was familiar with photography because my father is a professional photographer, and as a child I had spent many hours watching him work in his darkroom. The photography class pushed back the boundaries of visual experience for me. I learned that realism is only one of many styles of visual expression. I began to take pictures, and I started to think about telling a story with photographs and written narrative. (I wasn't interested in movies or video then, but later, in 1980, I did make the movie *Estoymuut and the Gunnadeyah* [Arrowboy and the Witches], which is an experiment with storytelling on film.) At the same time, I enrolled in a graduate English class that proposed to explore the relationships between texts and the visual images accompanying the texts. We were looking at the watercolors and texts of William Blake, but the direction the inquiry took was not at all the direction that I had imagined, so I dropped the class, and I dropped out of graduate school around that time too. But I never stopped thinking about the relationship between the text and visual images that accompany the text.

The tension between the word and the image goes back thousands of years in Europe and the Middle East. Of course written words are visual images, but in the West, the texts and the illustrations have had an uneasy and unequal relationship on the page. The old fear of idolatry kept visual images apart from texts except as embellishments put to the service of the text. Over time, the balance of power shifted and the visual image dominated, and the text merely served to announce the name or the source of the visual image. In Western tradition, there appear to be few instances of harmonious or balanced relationships between the text and the illustrations. Except for William Blake's works, only certain children's books approach a harmony between word and picture, and it is revealing that in Western culture, children's literature is not taken seriously.

In Asia, where writing is ideographic and descends originally from picture writing, such conflicts between text and picture do not exist. The old Chinese saying that a picture is worth a thousand words is misunderstood by Westerners. At the time the saying originated, the term *picture* included the ideograms that formed the text or poem within the painting. For the old Chinese, writing *was* a picture. Westerners came to misinterpret the old Chinese saying because they wanted to believe that a photograph was a fact, that a photograph revealed reality and could not lie.

We have known almost from the start that photographs, while they don't exactly lie (unless the negative has been tampered with or electronically enhanced), depend upon words, spoken or written, to identify the location or the occasion or the subject photographed. We are shown a film or video image of a hospital nursery with overturned and empty incubators. Without words, we don't know where this nursery is and we don't know what has happened. Network television tells us that what we see is Kuwait where Iraqi soldiers have dumped Kuwaiti babies out of incubators. The woman in the video image says she is a nurse who witnessed the act. Later on, when Desert Storm has ended, we learn that the hospital nursery scenes with the overturned incubators were completely fabricated.

I am interested in the effect that a photograph or other

visual image has on our reading of a text. *Sacred Water* is my experiment. Whereas the goals of photographers of the realism school are to make pictures that speak for themselves or speak a thousand words or tell a story themselves, I am interested in photographic images that obscure rather than reveal; I am intrigued with photographs that don't tell you what you are supposed to notice, that don't illustrate the text, that don't serve the text, but that form a part of the field of vision for the reading of the text and thereby become part of the reader's experience of the text. The influence of the accompanying photographic images on the text is almost subliminal.

The text of *Sacred Water* was composed so that the words do not overpower the odd minimalism of the pictures but instead depend upon the pictures for a subtle resonance. I take my photographs and print them on a laser copying machine in the "photo" mode; the resulting image is more stark and abstract than a traditional photographic print, which tends to dominate the page regardless of the text.

I was tired of the big publishers after the book tours for *Almanac of the Dead,* and I decided not even to bother showing my prototype of *Sacred Water* to my editor at Simon & Schuster. I wanted to have complete control over the book, from the design of the book to the actual sewing and gluing of the book. The appearance of the book itself forms part of the reader's experience of the text. I make the books for the sheer sensual pleasure of the paper, glue, and the copy machine images of my photographs. Hand-set type is wonderful, but it wouldn't be right for this book. I want a book that is unmistakably my book, a book that only I could make. The handmade copies of *Sacred Water* look as if a fifth-grade child sewed and glued them; and indeed, while I am sewing and gluing the books, I feel magically transported back to the blissful consciousness of a fifth-grader.

In the sixth grade I got into a lot of trouble when I wrote down a dirty joke. All the sixth-graders and most of the fifth-graders had been telling the joke to one another. Since I came from a community with the tradition of the spoken, not the written word, why was it that I felt compelled to write down this joke? The adjustment to the new school in Albuquerque had been difficult and I was anxious to be accepted by my new classmates. We sixth-graders knew that we might be reprimanded for telling the joke at school, but no one was really afraid to tell it. That was why I thought it would be a simple matter to write down this joke and to start a joke magazine that I would circulate around the sixth grade.

I painstakingly handprinted two copies of my magazine, which I named appropriately *Nasty Asty.* I decorated the pages of my magazine with the little black silhouette figures of *Playboy* playmates with bunny tails and bunny ears that adorned the joke page in *Playboy* magazine. I remember that I considered cutting out pictures of bare breasts to adorn the pages of *Nasty Asty;* I knew the boys in my sixth-grade class would be delighted if I did. But even then I knew the color magazine photographs of bare breasts would overpower and take too much attention away from the text. Also, the focus of the joke was on the male anatomy, not the female anatomy, and that may have been why I decided to publish the joke. Already I had noticed that in the world outside Laguna, a great deal of humor came at the expense of the female anatomy; at Laguna, the male anatomy got equal attention.

The Pueblo communities of my childhood had a very relaxed, broadminded outlook on the human body and sexuality; at home, my parents had a very liberal attitude toward nudity and sex. My father subscribed to *Playboy* magazine, and from Book-of-the-Month Club he ordered *Lady Chatterley's Lover* and *Lolita* when they were finally published in the United States. We were allowed to read any book or magazine in the house. My mother used to make jokes about the pages full of women's breasts, so we knew not to take *Playboy* magazine too seriously.

Maybe I was beginning to understand that in the dominant culture, the written word carries far more weight and authority than the spoken word, and I wanted to test this power when I wrote down this joke:

> *Mr. Bennett called his pretty secretary into his office to go over some reports she had been typing for him. He got close to her, then suddenly took her in his arms and unzipped his trousers. Just as he tried to lift her dress, the telephone in the outer office rang, and the pretty secretary ran to answer the phone with Mr. Bennett running after her. She slammed the door behind her, and there was a loud scream; the secretary called out, "Oh Mr. Bennett!" And her boss yelled, "Bent it? Goddamn it, I broke it!"*

I remember how much effort was required to make two copies of my joke magazine. I cut and pasted late into the night, far past the time I usually spent at my desk doing homework. The next day I took my two copies of *Nasty Asty* to school, and they were a great success among the entire sixth grade, except for Helen Grevey, who went home and told her mother. Suddenly I found out how seriously the written word is taken; I was called into the principal's office. But my classmates were very loyal and they went in a delegation to the school principal, Mrs. Westerfield, and told her that everyone had been telling the joke and that I had only written down what I had heard. I think my classmates saved me from expulsion, because Mrs. Grevey was a woman to be reckoned with.

I was sewing and gluing covers for copies of *Sacred Water* when I remembered my sixth-grade misadventure in publishing. I recalled that night long ago when I cut and pasted the two copies of *Nasty Asty* magazine, all the while anticipating the delight of my classmates when they saw what I had made. The handmade copies of *Sacred Water* even evoke the cut-and-paste media of a sixth-grader. Surely the origins of Flood Plain Press extend all the way back to my sixth-grade experiment.

Much has been made of the immutability of the text; once written down or published, the text, supposedly, did not change and thus could be relied upon. The spoken word and oral literatures were considered to be of lesser value, allegedly because spoken words were more likely to be forgotten or changed. But copyists and editors have been changing words in written texts since before the birth of Christ. One has only to look at the volumes of corrections and emendations of James Joyce's texts or the ever-shifting English translations of Marcel Proust to realize that the written word is no more and no less reliable than the spoken word.

One of the chief advantages of publishing my own books is that the written texts may continue to evolve in somewhat the fashion of oral texts. When I see a word or phrase or a punctuation in *Sacred Water* that I don't like, I simply change it the next time I run off a hundred copies of *Sacred Water.* So far I have received two letters, both from concerned professors who carefully listed all the errors they found in the first edition of *Sacred Water.* Here is an excerpt from my reply to one of the letters:

Thank you so much for your letter with the list of misspellings and punctuation flubs, plus the missing article "a" on page 66. I am currently retyping the entire text of Sacred Water *for the second edition, and your corrections came just in time to be part of the second edition. I am a terrible proofreader, a worse typist, and a hopeless speller. The alleged spelling-correction mode in my word processor is useless. Nonetheless, I decided that I would publish this book myself; I didn't even bother to show it to my agent or the "big publishers" because I knew they would whine about the odd format.*

Now that you have so generously and graciously provided help with the proofreading, Sacred Water *has taken on a bit of the communal, collaborative spirit that informs the old storytelling tradition. Listeners are expected to speak up if they discern a lapse in the storyteller's rendition or if they possess a variation of the story. Of course, spelling and punctuation errors are no problem in the oral tradition.*

I have always been intrigued with the history of spelling in England and the United States. It was Noah Webster who sought to standardize spellings, pronunciations, and usages in the U. S. so that the regional and ethnic differences among the thirteen original states might be minimized. Webster's first dictionary was intended to "homogenize" this country.

I love reading the writers of the Elizabethan Age because in those days, individuals were proud to coin their own variations on the spelling of a word. Eccentric spellings were thought to be evidence of imagination and wit. So I have to admit to being a bit of an Elizabethan in this regard.

I have tried to get rid of the spelling and punctuation errors, but the forces of entropy are always at work. Each time I retype a page and make corrections, OTHER *insidious little errors appear in areas that previously were error free. For this reason, I have no intention of publishing the work of other writers at Flood Plain Press. I do not wish to be responsible for the texts of other writers; the responsibility is too large. The big publishers send out books that are full of all sorts of errors despite big staffs and big machines. With Flood Plain Press, I have no one to blame but myself. When errors occur, they are* MY *errors, which are more interesting than a stranger's errors. Scholars with Freudian interests may find all sorts of revealing "slips" in my lapses, whereas such errors by Simon & Schuster reveal nothing.*

This new second edition will number 2,500 copies, which I have designed and typed for the printers. The full color cover is also my design. These copies from the printers will not be quite the same as the handmade copies of *Sacred Water*,[1] but they will make *Sacred Water* more available and affordable for students.

The Indian with a Camera

PETROGLYPHS ON ROCK outcrops along the San Jose River suggest that the paleo-Indian ancestors of the Pueblos had already begun to make images of spiritual significance on the sandstone eighteen thousand years ago. Pueblo kivas have stylized abstract designs painted on the walls and altarpieces. The Pueblo people had long understood that certain man-made visual images were sacred and were necessary to Pueblo ceremony.

The Pueblo people did not fear or hate cameras or the photographic image so much as they objected to the intrusive vulgarity of the white men who gazed through the lens. My grandfather Henry Marmon attended Indian school in Riverside, California, which might explain his fascination with and purchase of a snapshot camera in the 1920s. As a child in the 1950s, I remember the delight of bringing out the old Hopi basket with the grasshopper-man design, because Grandma Lily kept all of Grandpa Hank's snapshots and all the other family snapshots in the tall Hopi basket.

My sisters and cousins and I were too young to recognize the old-time people in the photographs, although we often recognized mesas and hills and certain houses. And so it was necessary that any viewing of the old snapshots in the Hopi basket be accompanied by a running commentary by my father and Grandma Lily, although they sometimes had to ask Grandpa Hank to help identify the really old Laguna people long dead and gone. The identification of the faces and the places in the photographs never failed to precipitate wonderful stories about the old days, which in turn brought out even older stories that stretched far beyond the confines of the snapshots in the grasshopper basket.

Our family is of mixed Laguna and white ancestry, but as a child I saw that many of the homes of the most traditional and conservative Laguna people included a great many photographs of family members.

At first, white men and their cameras were not barred from the sacred kachina dances and kiva rites. But soon the Hopis and other Pueblo people learned from experience that most white photographers attending sacred dances were cheap voyeurs who had no reverence for the spiritual. Worse, Pueblo leaders feared the photographs would be used to prosecute the caciques and other kiva members, because the United States government had outlawed the practice of the Pueblo religion in favor of Christianity exclusively.

Pueblo people may not believe that the camera steals the soul of the subject, but certainly the Pueblo people are quite aware of the intimate nature of the photographic image. Because Pueblo people appreciate so deeply the power and significance of the photographic image, they refuse to allow strangers with cameras the outrages to privacy that had been forced upon Pueblo people in the past.

Pueblo cultures seek to include rather than exclude. The Pueblo impulse is to accept and incorporate what works, because human survival in the southwestern climate is so arduous and risky. Before the Europeans appeared, the cultures of the Americas had vast networks of trade and commerce: during times of famine, trade partners sent food. Guatemalan macaw feathers went to Taos, and Minnesota pipestones to Honduras.

Europeans were shocked at the speed and ease with which Native Americans synthesized, then incorporated, what was alien and new. Mexican Indians had embraced Jesus, Mary, Joseph, and the saints almost at once; the Indians had happily set the Christian gods on their altars to join the legions of older American spirits and gods. The Europeans completely misread the inclusivity of the Native American worldview, and they were disgusted by what they perceived to be weakness and disloyalty by the Indians to their Indian gods. For Europeans, it was quite unimaginable that Quetzalcoatl might ever share the altar with Jesus.

Euro-Americans project their own fears and values in their perception of a conflict between Native American photographers and traditional native artists. Traditional artists reassure the Euro-Americans that, while not extinct, Native Americans are not truly part of American society. The Indian with a camera is frightening for a number of reasons. Euro-Americans desperately need to believe that the indigenous people and cultures that were destroyed were somehow less than human; Indian photographers are proof to the contrary.

The Indian with a camera is an omen of a time in the future that all Euro-Americans unconsciously dread: the time when the indigenous people of the Americas will retake their land. Euro-Americans distract themselves with whether a real, or traditional, or authentic Indian would, should, or could work with a camera. (Get those Indians back to their basket making!)

Euro-Americans desperately try to deny what has already begun, that inexorable force which has already been set loose in the Americas. Hopi, Aztec, Maya, Inca—these are the people who would not die, the people who do not change, because they are always changing. The Indian with a camera announces the twilight of Eurocentric America.

Pueblo people today are quite sophisticated about film and video technology. Like all human beings they are concerned with their continued survival as the people *they believe themselves to be.* What is essential to all Pueblo people is that generation after generation will continue to remember and to tell one another who they are, who they have been, and who they may become.

Pueblo narratives are not mere bedtime stories or light entertainment. Through the narratives Pueblo people have for thousands of years maintained and transmitted their entire culture; not all the strategies and beliefs necessary to Pueblo survival are written, but they are remembered and repeated generation after generation. Even the most ordinary deer-hunting story is dense with information, from stalking techniques to weather forecasting and the correct rituals to be performed in honor of the dead deer. In short, the stories and reminiscences that enliven all Pueblo social gatherings are densely encoded with expression and information.

When the United States government began to forcibly remove Pueblo children to distant boarding schools in the

1890s, the Pueblo people faced a great crisis. Like the slaughter of the buffalo, the removal of Native American children to boarding schools was a calculated act of cultural genocide. How would the children hear and see, how would the children learn and remember what Pueblo people, what Native Americans for thousands of years had known and remembered together?

But the calculations failed. Eventually the children were returned to their beloved sandstone and expanses of blue sky: again the place soaked them in, and they were reunited with what continues and what has always continued.

On Photography

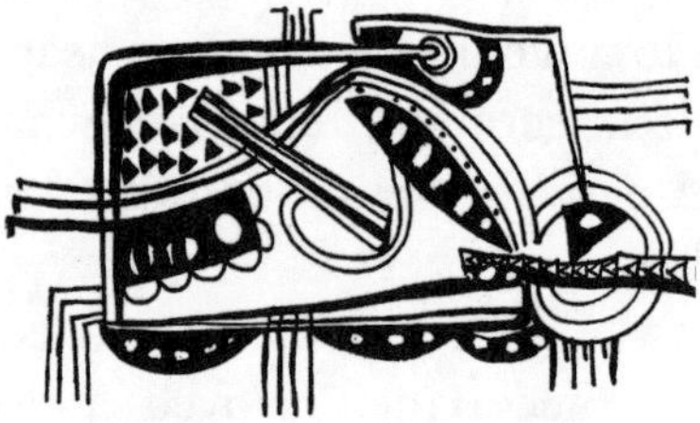

I HAVE BEEN around trays of developer and hypo under red safelights since I was old enough to perch on a high stool. My father, Lee H. Marmon, learned photography in the army. But to me it is still magic. The more I read about the behavior of subatomic particles of light, the more confident I am that photographs are capable of registering subtle electromagnetic changes in both the subject and the photographer. Professor Konomi Ara, my Japanese translator, photographed me outside my house in Tucson. Months later, when I saw the photograph in a Japanese publication, I was amazed and delighted to see how Japanese I appeared. How does this happen? Perhaps the way the photographer feels about her subject affects the outcome. Professor Ara had spent three years translating my novel *Ceremony* into Japanese; thus, in a few seconds, she was able to translate my face into Japanese.

Perhaps photographs register ambient bursts of energy in the form of heat or X rays as well as light. Thus photographs reveal more than a mere image of a subject, although it is still too early for us to understand or interpret all the information a photograph may contain. In the summer and fall of 1980, I felt strangely inclined to take roll after roll of black-and-white film with a cheap autofocus camera. Obsessively, I photographed the dry wash below my ranch house. Stone formations with Hohokam cisterns carved in them appeared as sacred cenotes, and flattop boulders looked as if they were sacrificial altars. Then, after the summer storms, I began to photograph certain natural configurations of stones and driftwood left by the floodwater. The photographic images of the stones and wood reminded me of glyphs. I could imagine there were messages in these delicate arrangements left in the wake of the flash flood. As I began to look at the prints, I realized each roll of film formed a complete photo narrative, although that had not been my intention as I pressed the shutter release. Most of these narratives were constructed from the images of the "glyphs" I "saw" in the debris in the bottom of the arroyo.

One roll of film is memorable and horrifying in the clarity of its photographic images: this roll narrates what I can only see now as the abduction and murder of a woman or child whose body is buried in a shallow grave in the desert. There is a menacing black sedan parked incongruously in the bottom of the dry wash near a trail; at the time I snapped the picture, the car did not seem ominous. And at the time I photographed the big spider web gleaming in the weeds at the base of an ocotillo, I had no idea how much like a sunken, shallow grave the spider web would appear on film.

The origin of waves or particles of light-energy that may give such a sinister cast to a photograph is as yet unexplained. Fields of electromagnetic force affect light. Crowds of human beings massed together emanate actual electricity. Individual perceptions and behavior are altered. Witnesses report feeling an "electricity" that binds and propels a mob as a single creature. So the greed and violence of the last century in the United States are palpable; what we have done to one another and to the earth is registered in the very atmosphere and effect, even in the light. "Murder, murder," sighs the wind over the rocks in a remote Arizona canyon where they betrayed Geronimo.

Geronimo was photographed immediately after his arrest in Skeleton Canyon. Cherokee artist Jimmie Durham writes, "Geronimo had the right to be hopeless and crazy, to be reduced to a passive beggar like so many Indian people at the time. Yet even when he was finally captured, he reportedly said, 'So you have captured me; the Mexicans would have killed me.' Then he looks at the camera, at the 'audience,' and tells us he will continue to resist." Durham chose to write about a photograph of Geronimo made after he had been imprisoned for years at Fort Sill, Oklahoma. In a fine top hat and vest, he sits behind the wheel of a new Cadillac. Durham writes, "Later, in the 20th century, when he is not allowed a rifle or his chaparral, he puts on your hat, takes the wheel, and stares the camera down. This photo makes clear that no matter what had been taken from him, he had given up nothing."

When Gerald McMaster looks at a photograph of students at a Canadian Industrial School for Indians, he sees that "these boys appear defiant. I was intrigued by their apparent ambivalence about being photographed, indicated by clenched fists or folded arms. Despite their cropped hair and foreign clothes, an element of individuality persists. . . . These boys represented the colonial experiment, a type of colonial alchemy, transforming the savage into a civilized human. Yet somehow their resistance remains visible."

A FEARLESS SCHOLAR who treads where few others dare, Lucy Lippard delights in stripping away comfortable images and clichés about photography and about Native Americans. In *Partial Recall,* she expands the aesthetic and perceptual boundaries of Western European art history as she invites twelve Native American artists and writers to write about the influences photographic images have had in the formation of Native American identity. Not since Susan Sontag's *On Photography* have there been such original and daring statements about photography—for instance, David Seals's discussions of sexism and racism in some Indian men. He admires the Scottish photographer Sarah Penman, who rides in subzero temperatures to photograph Wounded Knee riders commemorating the massacre. Seals's point is that the spiritual integrity of the person behind the camera matters most. The people of my great-grandmother's generation were concerned less with a person's ancestry than with a person's integrity. Generosity and honesty were always more important than skin color in the old days before so many terrible crimes were committed.

Victor Masayesva (quoted in the introduction) points out how the camera "worships" and honors the ancient spirit beings and sacred ceremonies by averting its eye, so that Hopi photographers display their reverence not only with the images they make, but also with the images they choose not to make. At Hopi, thoughtful action of any sort becomes worship; devoted attentiveness becomes worship. Ramona Sakiestewa writes with such beauty and passion about weaving that I imagined I had a flash of insight into the sensuous relationship the weaver enjoys with all the delicious textures. There is a difference between Jo Mora's intricate depictions and photographs by voyeurs/vampires like Curtis, Voth, and Vroman. That difference is love. Only one who loves Hopi weaving the way Sakiestewa does can see that Mora, too, loves weaving, that his photographs are a celebration of the beauty and complexity of the woven sashes and kilts, not some ethnographic document of the dancers' figures or actions.

Another of my favorite essays in *Partial Recall* is Rayna Green's brilliant explication of a Victorian-era photograph taken by a Japanese photographer of two Indian girls posed in the fashion of the day on a fainting couch. She gives us a witty recapitulation of the brief history of American Indians and the photographic image, concluding, "these ladies have got no small measure of bravado. And not the 'it's-a-good-day-to-die' kind. I appreciate that often necessary and brave machismo, given circumstances, but there might have been other ways of weathering the storm. These girls have got it. Matsura saw it. What's more, he took its picture."

Indians are changed, but in control, and not always poor either. Joy Harjo's delightful story about the photograph of Marsie Harjo at the wheel of the big Hudson he always drove reveals the diversity of Native American experience. Oil money made it possible for one generation of Harjos to live in luxury. Without this photograph we might forget that Marsie Harjo's wife, Katie, was descended from the great Muscogee leader Monahwee, and that the fertile farmlands of Alabama had made all the Muscogee people rich until the white man came.

Five hundred years after the Native American holocaust began with Columbus's arrival, too many of us Indians are still here. We all know the story: sixty to eighty million people died in the first one hundred years. But now Mexico City is the most populous city on earth, and the millions and millions who live there are Indians and mestizos. It is only a matter of time before the indigenous people of the Americas retake their land from the invaders, just as the African tribal people have repossessed nearly all the continent. Five hundred years is not much when compared to the fifteen thousand years Native Americans have lived on these continents. Thousands of years were necessary for the people to learn how to live *with* the land to survive and even thrive during the most difficult droughts and climate changes.

Great climatic changes are also under way today; on this point all can agree. Is it the greenhouse effect from fossil fuels, a consequence of aboveground nuclear tests, or is it simply another dimension of some ancient cycle of the earth? Los Angeles, Las Vegas, San Diego, Phoenix, and Tucson are cities in the desert; supplies of potable water for these cities are dwindling fast. Maybe the newcomers need another five hundred or even a thousand years to learn how to live with the earth here, but when the water has run out, their time will have run out too. Who will be left? Only a few remember how the desert nourishes her children who live with her. When they look at photographs of Los Angeles or Las Vegas, they will be amazed that the strangers lasted as long as they did.

FROM 1950 TO the present my father has photographed the land and the people of the Laguna-Acoma area. Sometimes the families of the old folks would ask him to come. He used available light because he knew the old folks would be more comfortable without flashes, so usually the photographs were made outside. The old-time people liked to spend most of their time outdoors anyway. My father liked to take informal portraits: the old man with his prize watermelon, the old woman with her oven bread on a board. He knew that these old folks, who had loved him and watched out for him as a child, would pass on to Cliff House soon. We all meet there at Cliff House someday, but I think my father couldn't bear to wait that long to see their beloved faces again.

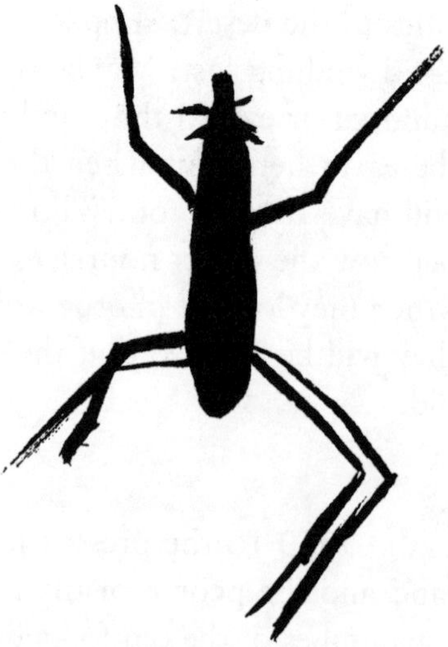

An Essay on Rocks

FROM THE TOP of the ridge I can see off in the distance a black form against the white arroyo sand. The first time I noticed it, my curiosity was aroused. I thought it had to be something—a blackened carcass or a floor safe half buried in the sand. Some days it appears to be the head of a horse, and other times it looks like a steamer trunk of black tin.

The arroyo descends through black basalt and pale ridges of crumbling volcanic tufa that are thick with jade green palo verde and giant saguaro that thrive where the ancient volcano exploded. The violence of the explosion destroyed the volcano, and all that remains are these weathered cone-shaped hills of dark lava and basalt layered with pale

ash. In the explosions, great fiery gaseous clouds sucked up pebbles and stones and melted them into strange glassy rocks with colorful swirls and patterns of stars.

After I leave the top of the ridge, I can no longer see the black object, only glimpses of the white sand of the arroyo snaking through the dark green thickets and black basalt. From time to time as I walk down the ridge through the palo verde and jojoba thicket, I try to locate the black object in the wash; but it can only be seen from the top of the ridge.

I make my way through the bright green cat's-claw and the leafy mesquites that border the wash, and as I get closer I try to anticipate what I will find. These lava hills northwest of Tucson are full of secrets. Loot from the last train robbery in 1917 was carried to these hills. Bootleggers brewed sour mash in the old mine shafts to avoid detection during Prohibition; rusty hoops from oak barrels are all that remain. Duffel bags full of cash and cocaine are heaved out of airplanes

in the middle of the night. Kidnappers scrape out shallow graves in the gravel; they cover their victims with dry weeds and debris; in time, the desert spiders spin thick webs over the weeds.

The palms of my hands are wet with anticipation. I glance over my shoulder from time to time to get my bearings from the top of the ridge. I must be almost there, I think. My alignment with the ridge is perfect.

I have watched the black form from the top of the ridge for months; still, what I see now seems much too small to be the black object I've been watching. Yet I am aligned with the ridge; this is the place. It is only a black rock the size of an

auto engine alone in the middle of the arroyo half buried in white sand. When it rains, the runoff water parts to flow around the black rock on either side. A small, umbrella-shaped mesquite tree grows beside the black rock.

Observed close up, the rock has a smooth metallic luster sometimes found on meteorites. It is a rock with the peculiar property of appearing larger at a distance and smaller when seen close-up. Those who pay no attention to rocks may be surprised, but the appearance of a rock may change from hour to hour. Some attribute the changes to the angle of the sun or the shift in shadows on the snow next to the rock. Once while I was deer hunting I saw a giant bear sleeping on a rock in the sun; when I got closer there was only the great basalt boulder amid the patches of melting snow.

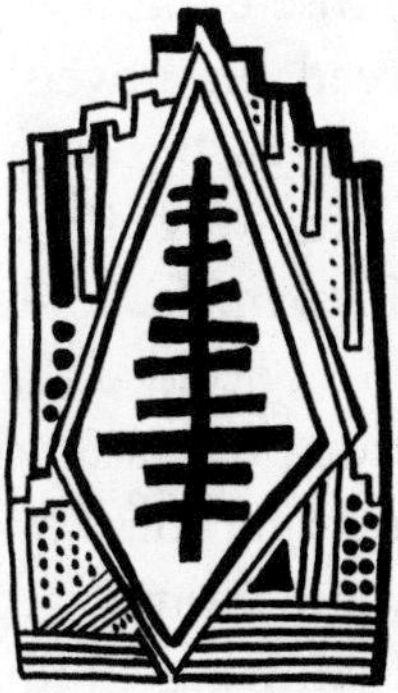

On Nonfiction Prose

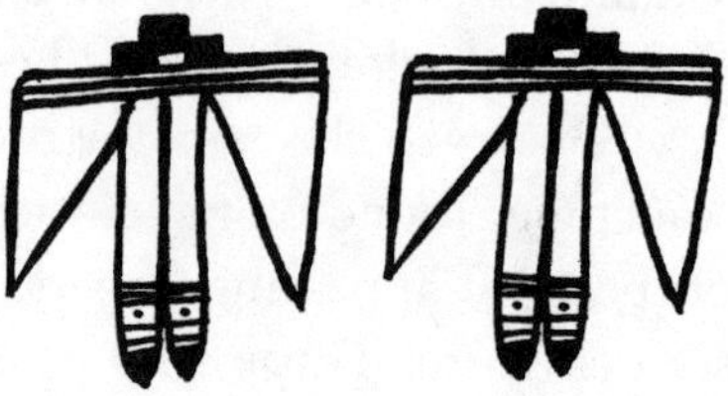

In my senior year as an English major at the University of New Mexico, I accidentally enrolled in a course on Victorian prose because for me the only prose was fiction. I expected to read the novels and stories of Rudyard Kipling and Frank Harris, but what I found when I looked at the list of class texts was Thomas Macaulay, Bishop Berkeley, and John Ruskin. I could have dropped the class and found another, but I decided that I would remain in the class because nonfiction prose seemed to me the most difficult genre to master. By reading these Victorian masters of the essay, I became even more intimidated by the prospect of writing nonfiction prose. Following graduation, I spent three semesters of writing answers to essay-style questions in law school. I developed the ability to compose essay-style answers at the keyboard against the clock, but I could feel the curriculum suck the life out of my imagination and out of my writing.

After I dropped out of law school, I wrote poetry and short fiction. I even wrote the novella *Hummaweepi the Warrior Priest* in the spring, summer, and fall of 1971 when I was pregnant with Cazimir. But I did not write nonfiction prose, not unless you count letters. Since I was six or seven years old I had loved to write letters to Grandma Jessie and Aunt Lucy. Although Aunt Lucy had come to stay with us at Laguna only four or five times during my childhood, still I feel a very close, loving connection with her because of our letters to one another through the years until she died. From Aunt Lucy I learned how a loving relationship may thrive with only the contact of letters. I have always loved to write letters.

The move to Chinle, Arizona, meant more letters to the family and friends I'd left behind in New Mexico, but it was the move to Ketchikan, Alaska, that marked the beginning of my longest letters to my friends Mei-Mei Berssenbrugge, Lawson Inada, and Simon Ortiz. I felt a terrible sense of isolation in that southeast Alaska town that dissolved when I read the letters my friends sent.

My correspondence with my friend Jim Wright began at a time when I was very much isolated after my move to Tucson. Jim Wright's letters were a lifeline to me, just as the letters from friends had saved me from despair before, in Alaska. What a loss we all suffered when Jim died. I could not have been as brave as Annie Wright was when she edited the book of our letters, *The Delicacy and Strength of Lace.* Even now, I have never read the book of our letters—occasionally I allow my eyes to rest on a page in the book as if to test myself, to see if the grief still chokes tears into my eyes.

The letters were important in my development as a nonfiction prose writer, but the reading I did was equally important. I especially appreciate Paul Valéry's *Leonardo, Poe, Mallarmé* and Elias Cannetti's *Crowds and Power,* and of course, "The Killing of a Porcupine" by D. H. Lawrence.

In the early 1980s, as I was beginning to write *Almanac of the Dead,* I began a series of short prose pieces about the desert area around my house and about the rocks and about the rain that is so precious to this land and to my household, which still depends on wells for all its water. In 1980 I had also begun to take photographs of the rocks in the big wash by my house; I used black-and-white and color film, and Polaroid film as well. I began collecting newspaper clippings and magazine articles about rocks that ran amok and about meteorites that fell through roofs. I began to save articles about rain, about the El Niño weather systems that cause floods in some areas and droughts in others. I began assembling piles of notes I had made on rocks and on rain. I intended to write two long essays, one on rain and one on rocks.

I have continued to gather and hoard piles of notes and articles for my essays. I imagined my essays as perfect pieces, and I did not want to hurry them. I set the notes and incomplete essays aside while I completed *Almanac.* I recall a section of the novel in which there are descriptions of the peculiar rocks in the Tucson Mountains.

But in the meantime I got requests to write essays, and sometimes, if the topic interested me, I would agree. Later, as I toiled over bland prose and argued with magazine editors, I would regret that I had ever agreed to write nonfiction and I would swear off nonfiction prose forever. But secretly I hoped that the struggle with other pieces of nonfiction would empower me to bring forth my essays on rain and on rocks. Instead, the writing of these other essays has had an unexpected effect on my essays about rain and about rocks, as you will see.

In my 1993 self-published book, *Sacred Water,* photocopies of my photographs of clouds and dry washes are an integral part of the text; the photocopy images are as much a part of my essay on water as the narrative of the essay. The Pueblo people have always connected certain stories with certain locations; it is these places that give the narratives such resonance over the centuries. The Pueblo people and the land and the stories are inseparable. In the creation of the text itself, I see no reason to separate visual images from written words that are visual images themselves.

Old and New Autobiographical Notes

From the First Edition of *Laguna Woman*

I WAS BORN March 5, 1948 in Albuquerque, New Mexico. I grew up at Laguna in the house where my father was born. The house was built ninety years ago with rock and adobe mortar walls two feet thick. Outside there was a great old mountain cottonwood tree five feet around at its base. Our house was next to my great-grandmother's house. My mother had to work, so I spent most of my time with my great-grandma, following her around her yard while she watered the hollyhocks and blue morning glories.

When I got older I carried the coal bucket inside for her.

Her name was Maria Anaya, and she was born in Paguate village, north of Old Laguna. She came to Laguna when she married my great-grandfather, who was a white man. She took care of me and my sisters and she told us about how things were when she was a little girl.

The white men who came to the Laguna Pueblo reservation and married Laguna women were the beginning of the half-breed Laguna people like my family, the Marmon family. The Marmons are very controversial even now; but I think that people watch us more closely than they do full-bloods or white people. In the long run, we aren't much different from other Laguna families.

My mother was born in Montana, and her family came from a Plains Indian tribe; but she never knew which one for sure. My father stayed on the reservation and helped my grandpa and grandma with the little grocery store they had. My father was once elected treasurer of the Pueblo of Laguna, but being a Marmon, he didn't get along very well politically.

I suppose at the core of my writing is the attempt to identify what it is to be a half-breed, or mixed-blooded person; what it is to grow up neither white nor fully traditional Indian. It is for this reason that I hesitate to say that I am representative of Indian poets or Indian people. I am only one human being, one Laguna woman.

I attended the University of New Mexico and graduated in 1969. I went to law school at the University of New Mexico for three semesters before I dropped out to devote all my time to writing. I have a son, Robert, who was born in 1966, and another son, Cazimir, who was born in 1972. Presently, I am living with my husband, John Silko, in Ketchikan, Alaska, where I write fiction and poetry and he works as the supervising attorney for Alaska Legal Services.

BIOGRAPHICAL NOTE TO THE SECOND EDITION, AUTUMN 1994

TWENTY-ONE YEARS later, I sit in an old ranch house on a volcanic ridge northwest of Tucson, Arizona. My son Robert is a rare-book man at Booked Up in Archer City, Texas; my son Cazimir is a musician and writes science fiction in Tucson. While I was writing *Almanac of the Dead*, I learned to prefer solitude. A perfect day is a day spent watching my koi in their rainwater pool playing with the macaws, and writing, drawing, and reading.

I decided that I would make only a few revisions in the text of *Laguna Woman* for this second edition. I had to struggle with myself because I am capable of revising the life right out of a piece of writing. If I had allowed myself to get started, I might have rewritten all the poems entirely, and they'd have been ruined.

There were a great many typographical errors in the first edition of *Laguna Woman*. Just recently, while typesetting this edition, I noticed another error, which I had not noticed before, in my 1973 biographical note. In the fourth paragraph the word should be *grandmother,* not *mother.* It was my paternal grandmother, Grandma Lily, who knew only that her father's family were part Plains Indian, but she never knew which tribe. Grandma Lily's father, Grandpa Stagner, was half German, but his mother was an Indian woman named Rhoda Touchstone. Her death is recorded at the courthouse in Sweetwater, Texas. Grandma Lily's mother, Grandma Helen, was from the Romero family in Los Lunas. Her father was an Englishman named Whittington. Grandma Helen spoke Spanish.

My mother's mother was part Cherokee through her Grandfather Wood. Grandpa Wood was born somewhere in

Kentucky during the time the Cherokees were forced to march the Trail of Tears to Oklahoma. In North Carolina, there are Cherokees who still go by the name Wood. We were fortunate enough to meet our cousin Charlie Wood years ago when he worked for the Indian Public Health Service in the Laguna-Acoma area. My Grandma Jessie's sister, Aunt Lucy, used to come stay with us at Laguna. She told me what little she knew about our Cherokee ancestors.

When I was only in the fourth grade, Aunt Lucy gave me a lovely leather-bound copy of Longfellow's *Hiawatha.* I remember the leather smelled wonderful, and the pages held the lingering scent of the lavender from Aunt Lucy's suitcase. How I loved to rub my fingers across the gilded edges of the pages, which were shiny and smooth. Aunt Lucy wrote me beautiful letters and told me as much as she knew about Grandpa Wood and his sister, who died in Oklahoma.

I once felt distant from my Cherokee ancestors; but over the years, I have come to realize that the spirits of all our ancestors are limitless, and they range all across the American continents regardless of the years or the boundary lines. When I met the principal chief of the Cherokee Nation, Chief Wilma Mankiller, and her husband, Charlie Soap, last year, I felt a warmth and ease, as if I were home. We met in southwestern Virginia, also ancestral land of the Cherokee.

I used to wonder why the first edition of *Laguna Woman* was so riddled with typographical and other errors. I remember looking over the galley proofs Joe Bruchac sent from Greenfield Review Press; I even remember making corrections and changes on the galleys. What happened? I don't know. Nineteen seventy-three was a difficult year. There was a great deal of emotional turmoil in my life; I was trying to adjust to the rainy Alaskan coast. I imagine the galley proofs must have arrived during some crisis or another, when my negligible abilities as a proofreader were impaired. But how did I miss that glaring error of the word *mother* instead of the correct word *grandmother*? (My grandmothers and Great-grandma A'mooh were like mothers to me, it is true.)

The text of this second edition is substantially the same text that appears in the first edition. But like the spoken word, the written word also undergoes inexorable change through time. Much has been made about oral narratives, which may differ slightly with each performance. But the written word isn't immutable either; the endless revisions of the texts of Joyce and Proust illustrate this process.

I understand now that human communities are living beings that continue to change; while there may be a concept of the "traditional Indian" or "traditional Laguna Pueblo person," no such being has ever existed. All along there have been changes; for the ancient people any notions of "tradition" necessarily included the notion of making do with whatever was available, of adaptation for survival. Human beings have lived along the San Jose River for more than twenty thousand years; the people hunted the great mammoths until they disappeared, and gradually as the great herds of elk and bison shifted north, the people took up the dry farming of corn and beans, and they domesticated turkeys. Life continually changes.

Anthropologists have predicted the end of the indigenous people of the Americas for a long time. Yet this year my father was amazed to see how many deer dancers there were in the plaza at Old Laguna. Seventy-five or eighty deer dancers, more deer dancers than my father had ever seen before.

Acknowledgments

"Interior and Exterior Landscapes: The Pueblo Migration Stories" was first published in *Antaeus,* no. 57 (Autumn 1986).

"Language and Literature from a Pueblo Indian Perspective" was first published in *Critical Fictions,* edited by P. Mariani (Dia Foundation for the Arts, 1991).

"Yellow Woman and a Beauty of the Spirit" was first published in the *Los Angeles Times* Sunday magazine, December 29, 1994.

"America's Debt to the Indian Nations: Atoning for a Sordid Past" was first published in the *Los Angeles Times,* Sunday op-ed page, July 12, 1981.

"Auntie Kie Talks About U.S. Presidents and U.S. Indian Policy" was first published in *Mother Jones* magazine, October 1984, "Imagine Another Four Years of Reagan" issue.

"Hunger Stalked the Tribal People" was written for *The People's Tribune,* Thanksgiving 1994 issue, Chicago.

"Fences Against Freedom" was first published in *The Hungry Mind Review,* no. 31 (Fall 1994).

"The Border Patrol State" was first published in *The Nation,* October 26, 1994.

"Fifth World: The Return of Ma ah shra true ee, the Giant Serpent" was first published in *Artforum* (Summer 1989).

"Tribal Prophecies" was first published in the art exhibit catalog *Encuentro: Invasion of the Americas and the Making of the Mestizo,* December 1991, SPARC, Venice, California.

"Stone Avenue Mural" was first published by *City Lights Press* in its special issue on the Zapatista uprising, 1994.

"An Expression of Profound Gratitude to the Maya Zapatistas" was first published in *The People's Tribune,* February 29, 1994.

"The Indian with a Camera" was first published in a slightly different form in *Aperture,* no. 119 (Early Summer 1990).

"On Photography" was first published in *Partial Vision,* edited by Lucy Lippard (The Free Press, 1992).

Notes

Interior and Exterior Landscapes: The Pueblo Migration Stories

1. By *ancient Pueblo people* I mean the last generation or two, which included my great-grandmother, just barely. Their worldview was still uniquely Pueblo.

2. A *clan* is a social unit that is composed of families who share common ancestors and trace their lineage back to the Emergence, where their ancestors allied themselves with certain plants, animals, or elements.

3. *Ka'tsinas* are spirit beings who roam the earth and inhabit kachina masks worn in Pueblo ceremonial dances.

4. Chaco Culture National Historical Park is located in northwest New Mexico, about twenty-four road miles southwest of Nageezi on Highway 57.

5. The term *hummah-hah* refers to a traditional genre of storytelling at Laguna Pueblo.

6. Laguna and Paguate villages are about forty miles west of Albuquerque in the Laguna Indian reservation. Highway 279 links the two villages. Laguna and Zuñi Pueblos are the largest of the nineteen contemporary pueblos (eighteen are in New Mexico, plus the Hopi in Arizona). The Pueblo people are descendants of the Anasazi, who lived over a vast area of the Colorado Plateau half a millennium and more ago.

7. *The Emergence:* all of the human beings, animals, and life that had been created emerged from the four worlds below, when the earth was habitable. *The Migration:* the Pueblo people emerged into the Fifth World, but they had already been warned they would have to travel and search to find the place where they were meant to live. The *Fifth World* is the world we live in today. There are four previous worlds below this world.

8. *Creation:* Tse'itsi'nako, Thought Woman, the Spider, thought about it, and everything she thought came into being. First she thought of three sisters for herself, and they helped her to think of the rest of the Universe, including the Fifth World and the four worlds below.

9. The narratives indicate that the Migration from the north took many years. But the Emergence Place north of Paguate village is only eight miles from Laguna village, the place where the people finally settled. What can it mean that hundreds of years and hundreds of narratives later the Laguna people had traveled but eight miles? Anthropologists attempt to interpret the Emergence and Migration stories lit-

erally, with the Pueblo people leaving Chaco Canyon and Mesa Verde to go south to the Rio Grande Valley and to the mountains around Zuñi (south of Gallup, New Mexico, on the Arizona border).

Although traditional anthropologists allege otherwise, archaeological evidence will someday place human beings in the Western hemisphere from the very beginning.

THE BORDER PATROL STATE

1. The Treaty of Guadalupe Hidalgo, signed in 1848, recognizes the right of the Tohano O'Odom (Papago) people to move freely across the U.S.-Mexico border without documents. A treaty with Canada guarantees similar rights to those of the Iroquois nation in traversing the U.S.-Canada border.

AS A CHILD I LOVED TO DRAW AND CUT PAPER

1. The handmade editions are covered with Stephen Watson's Blue Corn paper, which is made in Albuquerque, and actually contains bits of blue corn. A limited edition was covered in Watson's white Volcanic Ash paper, which contains small amounts of fine ash obtained from the volcanos just west of Albuquerque.